"A  exactly that! This book is an experience."

—Mona Stevens
 Former Head Softball Coach, University of Utah
 Former USA Softball National Team Coach

"Jane's unique skill is being able to show you a guide to how you can change your life. In this book, Jane shows us how important it is to know our life plan and to live on purpose. Jane has personally coached me on these techniques. I am now living my life purpose, and enjoying every minute of it!"

—Mike Rogers
 Author, *The A to Z Guide to Alternative Medicine*

"With the life plan we sketched out as a compass by which to begin each day, I find myself inspired with greater frequency. The key for me was the recognition of ego and its ability to drag us down into bitterness. Fear, loathing, and negative self-talk have given way to a deeper sense of belonging to a larger intelligence. Our work together enabled me to align myself with this energy and be of service to something larger than my ego demands."

—Evan Duby
 Words With Management

The personal life plan of

_____

*When you are born,
your work is placed in your heart.*

—Kahlil Gibran, Lebanese-American poet

The Guide

**Knowing
the
Plan
for
Your Life**

Jane Miner, Ed.D.

PERSONAL Solutions
An imprint of Performance Publications
Ivins, Utah, USA

Copyright ©2007 Jane Miner

All rights reserved worldwide. Published and distributed in the United States of America. Except for the inclusion of brief quotations in articles and reviews, no part of this book may be copied, reproduced, or transmitted in any form or by any means without prior written permission from the publisher. For information, contact:

PERSONAL Solutions
140 Tuacahn Drive, #59 • Ivins, Utah, USA 84738
books@personalwisdom.net
435-688-7578

ISBN 13: 978-1-887476-04-1
ISBN 10: 1-887476-04-0
Library of Congress Control Number: 2007923363

Publishing Services provided by Jorlan Publishing:
Editing by Lana Jordan
Book Cover Design by Paula Tarver Leckey and Jill Ronsley
Book Layout and Design by Marny K. Parkin
www.JorlanPublishing.com

IMPORTANT: This book is intended to be used as a general guide for educational and entertainment purposes only. It is distributed with the understanding that the author and publisher shall have neither liability nor responsibility to any person or entity with respect to any loss or damage caused, or alleged to have been caused, directly or indirectly by the information provided herein.

Every effort has been made to assure accuracy, and to the best of our knowledge, all information and strategies contained in this book represent reliable facts and findings, and the honest and true insights of the author based on her personal and professional experience, knowledge, and research.

The author and publisher do not presume to engage in dispensing medical or psychological advice, and assume no responsibility or liability for any negligence or actions on the part of the reader relevant to this material. Information and strategies in this book are not intended to be used as substitutes for the services of a mental health specialist, counselor, or any other professional care in relationships, career transitions, or life changes.

If you do not wish to be bound by the above, you may return this book in new condition to the publisher for a full refund.

To you who have thought or felt
there was something unique and passionate
intended for your life.

It is time to know.

Contents

Acknowledgments	9
Prologue	13
Is There a Plan for You?	17
Why *The Guide*?	21
Using *The Guide*	27
The Truth About You (You'll Like It!)	31
Your Path to Joy with Love	37
The Components of *Your* Life Plan	43
Your Personal Life Vision	49
Your Personal Life Purpose	57
Your Personal Life Mission	75
Your Personal Gifts	93
Your Personal Standards	121
Your Personal Ego-Mind	157
Life on the Path	193
Ten Tips for Living Your Life on the Path	205
Working Your Life Plan	233
Back to the Beginning	245

Acknowledgments

A deep level of appreciation goes to many people who made this book and the life plan discovery process possible. Thank you to my many colleagues, clients, and students who in their own way supported the discovery and exploration of my life plan. On reflection, I know that all of them and the experiences we shared made the development of this process necessary and important. This includes the challenging and disappointing experiences as well as the illuminating and subtle ones. I now see their connection to bringing me to the writing of this book and the work I do. Most importantly, I may never have fully known my life plan without them.

Specifically, I want to acknowledge the owners and staff at the Green Valley Spa in St. George, Utah, who for six years have provided a rich and supportive environment for me to develop and learn about life plans. I am especially grateful to my many clients with whom

I have shared this process, for they helped me discover the concepts, questions, and process that *The Guide* now shares. Many of them now follow their life plans, making powerful impacts on people and the world while living passionate, joyful, and loving lives.

On a more personal level, I want to thank my parents, who recognized I had a direction for my life that they didn't know or understand at the time. They didn't know about life plans, but they did know to love and support who I was and potentially could be. I also want to thank my best friend, Cindy Carlson, who for thirty years has supported my wanderings with her trust, love, and searching questions—always accepting of my quirky answers. Like my parents, she chose to honor my potential with little judgment and incredible encouragement. She has also been a relentless editor for the thousands of pages I have written over the years. Her questions and corrections of what was written always made what I wrote better and often saved me from simple to complex typing and writing errors.

A special thanks to Cindy Clemens, my trusted life-coaching colleague, for her valued feedback on the book and especially for making sure that the life plan process worked. The first time Cindy and I met to discuss our work as life coaches, we talked about personal gifts and identified hers. Since that meeting years ago, she has been sharing her gifts and personal life plan to help people find joy and love their lives. Her insights and suggestions on the book were invaluable. Additionally, Dianne Marius of the Green Valley Spa was very helpful in reading the book to discover her life plan and then offering suggestions for clarity to make the process easier to follow.

Expert help came from Lana Jordan of Jorlan Publishing, along with Paula Tarver Leckey, Marny Parkin, and Jill Ronsley, who designed and published *The Guide* into a book that is attractive and useful. Lana's patient and professional editing of the manuscript made it so much clearer and more effective. All their suggestions and ability to capture the vision for the book made it easier to bring that vision to life.

In advance, I thank the readers who will use this process to change their lives and the lives of others. I am confident that in your discovery of your life plan and putting your compass to work, you will passionately affirm this process and the power of "knowing your life plan" to live fully in joy with abundant love. I look forward to benefiting from your efforts to slide your piece of the life puzzle into place, helping the world expand the joy and love intended for all of us and thereby fulfilling the *Promise* of all our life plans.

Prologue

Most people want to know their life plan because they are unhappy or disappointed with their current work or career. Some feel guilty that they have given so much time and energy to their work and now don't enjoy it anymore. They question why they chose it at all.

As unpleasant as this may feel, it is a great place to be because it can motivate people to explore and discover their life plan. It forces people to stop, re-evaluate where they are and what they are doing, and look for something more.

However, this opportunity and motivation can be lost when people make one common mistake: they move quickly to reduce the pain, guilt, and dissatisfaction by looking for an immediate change in their line of work or their workplace.

Such a change usually leads to the same conditions within a few months or a few years at best, because they haven't addressed the true source of their distress: not knowing or not following their life plan and/or being in a work environment that doesn't support their plan.

For maximum long-term results, the best approach would be to use the current opportunity and motivation to discover and explore their life plan. This can lead people to work that more closely aligns with who they are and what they were intended to do.

Work or a career will take up the majority of our time, effort, and energy over the course of a lifetime. Much of that work will be an expression of our true selves. However, if the work and the work environment don't align enough with who we are, we will become stressed and bored. Eventually, we will look for another work situation.

Doing work or following a career that aligns with our life plan is crucial for our joy, health, and wealth. The cost of misalignment is the loss or absence of our passion as well as damage to our physical, mental, emotional, and spiritual well-being.

It may take years to reach this point because people will tolerate the stress and unhappiness in order to earn an income—especially a high income. People justify this continuing sacrifice as the price they pay to work and make money in society. They are afraid to take a risk to find out if more is possible and intended for them. They often feel trapped by their training, experience, and fear of change.

Since you have picked up this book and are reading this prologue, it is likely that you are looking to make a change in your work or career or, you may be looking to find direction in your life. If so, it is time to know your life plan. It will be the springboard to passion and joy and work you love!

Is There a Plan for You?

You are reading this page because you either know or hope there is a plan for your life. Congratulations, there is a plan for you and every other human being! Your plan arrived with you at birth as the navigational tool for guiding your life, making choices, and creating experiences; it was intended to be your compass guiding you to a life filled with love and joy.

At times throughout your life you have known there was something important intended for you, as your unique life plan called to you in a flash of inspiration, a dream, or an attraction to something or someone. For many people it has been described as a feeling of something inside that gnawed at them. Even though you may have ignored this call or pushed it aside as impractical or idealistic, the plan waited patiently for you to discover and follow it.

By the end of this book you will know your life plan or have a very good idea what comprises it. Your plan will be a compass, pointing perfectly in the direction of the powerful life you were born to live, including the best and right choices for you to make each day.

There is one source for your plan and all life plans. Called by many names, this source is the same source that created you and placed life in you. Many call this source God, or the Creator. Some call it the Universe, the Source, or the Higher Self. By any name, it is the powerful source of everything there is and everything that is possible.

However, this is not a book about religion or even spirituality. It is a book about anything and everything in your life that you create through your choices, including your daily life, relationships, and work or career. Religious teachings and spiritual experiences should support and enhance your life plan, but they cannot provide it.

Your life plan is unique to you and you are the only one that can discover, explore, and live it. This plan is who you truly are, endowed by your creator to live your life in joy and love and help the world to do the same. Your intended life is powerful and profoundly sacred.

You will have plenty of help and resources for living your intended life and following your plan, but you and only you will decide what is helpful and supportive and what is not, relying on your personal compass to show you the way. The more you discover who you truly are and what you are alive to do, the more adept you will become at reading your compass. It is and will be the perfect guide, because it is *your* guide. The world needs you to firmly grasp your compass by knowing your plan and share yourself with us.

Martha Graham, one of the most innovative and creative dancers of all time and often called the mother of modern dance, said it perfectly, "There is a vitality, a life force, an energy, a quickening, that is translated through you into action, and because there is only one of you in all times, this expression is unique."

Why *The Guide?*

Sooner or later each of us asks ourselves the universal question, "Who am I?" This question is often followed by a related question, "What is the meaning of my life?" These are big questions looking for big answers. The answers are big, but clear. In fact, the answers to both questions are the same. *Your life has a purpose and that purpose will give full meaning to your life.*

I started asking these big questions about twenty-five years ago. Finding the answers started me on a long and winding journey. I thought often about what I did successfully and what I enjoyed doing. I also thought about when I was miserable and feeling lost. Those thoughts and reflections led me to what I did that gave me joy and gave meaning to my life. Throughout the process, I was also curious about how it all fit together. Was life just one long, winding, and bumpy road with some smooth sections, or was there a smoother path my life was intended to follow? I concluded there must be a direction or path, and my choices would be clear and sensible if I knew what it was.

Over the years there were also glimpses and clues that there was something holding it all together, possibly even a plan. When I started to see connections and relationships between my choices, efforts, and results, clarity started to emerge; there was a plan! The sooner I knew that plan and the path it was directing, the fewer years of wandering, frustration, and confusion I would have to navigate. Most importantly, I could live a purposeful life, rich with meaning.

I read books about life purpose and listened to people talk about purpose and meaning. The search to find the plan was not unique, nor new. Throughout history most, if not all people sooner or later had asked, "Who am I and what is the meaning of my life?" Of course, there were plenty of ideas and people willing to supply answers. Sometimes the answers were applied to a group; other times they were left as mysteries for individuals with directions to go this or that way. I continued to seek and ask the questions, now knowing they were also being asked somewhere by someone else.

Fortunately for me, I discovered most of the answers to who I was and what my life was meant to be. As I chose the path those answers directed, more was revealed. The more I knew, the more I knew what I was meant to do, who I was meant to be, and how I was to share it with the world. That led me to a process that I began to share with others so they could answer their two big questions as well. Now years later, that process has been refined and used by many people to explore and discover their personal paths for living the plan for their lives. That has brought you and me to these pages.

In this book called *The Guide*, I now share this powerful process with you. You can know your personal life plan and save yourself years of heartache, frustration, and disappointment, and especially, avoid the dreaded "living your life to please others" scenario.

Knowing your life plan will free you to be who you are and were meant to be, and to passionately share yourself with the world without needing permission or approval. When you complete *The Guide* you will be well on your way to living your life as it was intended—not to please others, but to love and serve them. Every day will have the potential for powerful meanings, delightful surprises, and magical experiences.

What can be a complicated process is simplified here to make it easy and accessible. It will take time, and the limitations of the written word may leave you befuddled now and then. But know this, the source of your life plan will always be available to clarify and guide you when the process in this book doesn't or can't. When you feel stuck or unclear, an experience will occur to show you where you need to go next, or something will be said to redirect you. The whole plan will be revealed to you if you stay open and keep following the process in this book. Best of all, when you know your plan it will fit on a 3x5" index card!

If you are alive, there is a life plan unique to you and your plan is connected to my plan and every other life plan. We are all part of a great puzzle called life. Each life and the plan for that life is an important piece in that puzzle.

If you don't know or follow the path directed by your plan, you will miss out and so will the world. When a piece of the puzzle is missing or lost, the puzzle is incomplete and the missing piece is sensed by all who want to experience the message of the puzzle. Yet, when another person slides their piece into the puzzle and a fit is made, we all share in that joy and love because it makes our pieces fit even better.

At no time in history has the life puzzle been more in need of the missing pieces. It is easy to look around and see a world where many people seem to be lost, with no idea that they are an important piece of a great puzzle. Their lives have no meaning because they don't know what is meaningful for them. They lack purpose because they don't know how necessary they are to the world. If they knew their unique plan, life would look very different and their experiences would change.

With this book and this process, I hope to help more people know their life plan, find the compass the plan provides, and put their piece of the life puzzle right where it belongs. That is what my plan has guided me to do here.

When you know your life plan, you will never have to worry about motivation, direction, or decisions. The plan will prompt you, call you, and never leave you alone. The plan will provide a clear focus for your choices because every choice will either align with your life plan or it won't.

Life will be simple, effortless, and deeply satisfying. You will no longer waste your time and energy with experiences, relationships, and work that don't allow you to express who you truly are. You will know what to do and how to do it, and you will want to do it. There will be you, your plan or compass, and a new day—every day.

The greatest part of knowing the plan for your life will be the power you feel. Some have called this your authentic power or the power within that arrived on earth with you. When used, this power will attract the people, opportunities, and resources for you to easily follow your plan and put your piece into the life puzzle. You will contribute to the authentic power of others and provide support for them to live a passionate life.

That is the point of your plan, my plan, and all other life plans. The world awaits you knowing what your powerful piece of the puzzle is and what to do with it, and so do I. *The Guide* will lead you to it.

Using *The Guide*

The Guide is designed to be done, not just read. This is a book written for you, about you. So did you write your name on the line provided on the first page of *The Guide*? If you didn't, please do it now. This small action symbolizes your ownership of your personal life plan and your commitment to the process of exploring, discovering, and living it. Go personalize your copy of the book and come back.

Using *The Guide* and following this process will take time, effort, and patience to discover who you were meant to be and how you were meant to live your life. Such a process can't be accomplished by just reading a book, even this book. Take your time, let it happen, and the process will unfold.

A lot is going to happen to you, around you, and in you while you are in this process. Experiences and interactions will be needed that can take weeks and even months. Some elements of the plan will not be revealed until after you have been living on the path of your plan. It will all be revealed in the order and at the time that is best for you.

You will be most successful by following the book as it is laid out, completing the exercises, and concluding with the important advice at the end of the book. If you try to read this book like you normally read a book, you will find it repetitive. There is repetition to facilitate the exploring of the plan and to continually tie the components together.

The book has an intentional flow that unfolds and reveals your plan as the process is followed. Additionally, the order of the components as presented is the best order for discovering your personal life plan. Skipping around and reading sections will not work well and may lead to confusion. Also, the book is designed to allow you to stop, leave it, and return where you left off. Most importantly, you will be asked to do this many times throughout the book.

This is a guide to discovering, exploring, and knowing the plan for your life and using that plan as the compass to direct your life path. When you reach the end you will be advised to return to the beginning to further refine your plan. Your plan and your life were intended to be a dynamic unfolding with continuing expansion. This will be even truer as you use your plan as a compass to guide your life path.

As you use your gifts, you will see how you are expressing your life purpose and sharing your life vision in what you choose to do each day. More depth, clarity, and power will be continually added to the plan and especially to daily living, as you tweak your plan after finding out what works most effectively for you and your interactions with the world. Over one hundred years ago, James Allen wrote a message as relevant today as it was then, "You cannot travel within and stand still without."

The Guide is your personal workbook to be completed, revised, and revisited often. It is recommended that you work through *The Guide* with a good pencil (or many pencils), as you will find yourself erasing and rewriting quite often. Once you get started, let your plan lead you.

You will get glimpses and clues as you consider the questions, write down your insights, and learn from the messages that will surround you. It won't take you years as it did me, but it will be an ongoing process that will require your focus and commitment.

Letting the process unfold cannot be emphasized enough. Be assured there is a plan for you and a path for you to follow from your plan. But it has many facets, necessary to move you along the path and return you to it when you wander away. The purpose of *The Guide* is to make it easy to navigate the path without costly diversions and distractions.

The necessary people and experiences with them and their paths will cross yours when it is time. The plan and the path cannot be hurried. They are not on your time, influenced by necessity, or bound by experiences. There is the best time; the time for you to discover, experience, and enjoy all you will attract.

So, if you find yourself stuck or frustrated with a component, question, or exercise, put *The Guide* down and come back later—even days later. While you are away from the discovery process, the information or answers you need will show up, sometimes as a terrific "aha" moment.

By the way, it helps to keep *The Guide* with you or in view while you are waiting for the information or experiences you need. This book will be your temporary plan and compass until you know your complete plan. You will want it with you and it is designed to easily go with you in your pocket, bag, or car.

Keep your focus on what *The Guide* is revealing, and your plan will be made known to you. Discover, experience, and enjoy it all as you go. The word "enjoying" means experiencing joy. And the sharing of your joy with love is the purpose of your life in the first and eventually, last place!

The Truth About You (You'll Like It!)

 Whenever people consider what they need or want to know about themselves, they are usually consumed with anxiety. Somewhere we were taught that the truth about ourselves is to be feared, hidden, and never explored, except when we needed to understand our weaknesses and shortcomings in order to improve ourselves. Then we were to painfully explore that dark part of ourselves; to cleanse and remove what was undesirable.

Usually this happened when life, a relationship, or work was frustrating, disappointing, or stressful and we felt helpless, conflicted, or even lost. We were told the answer was to change, and thus we had to explore that shadowy, dark inner self. Few of us wanted to go there and possibly feel even worse about ourselves—so we didn't.

The good news is that all those feelings and negative experiences weren't being caused by the deep and dark places you needed to explore. Instead, those feelings and experiences were indicators and even messages to you that you didn't know the plan for your life. Or if you knew, you were not following it.

Frustration, stress, conflict, guilt, and difficulties in situations are the result of not being true to who you really are and were intended to be. Your life was intended to be enjoyable, passionate, and deeply satisfying with each day bringing you joy and love. Anything else was a distraction or diversion from your intended life.

The truth about you is actually something you will like—a lot! People are always, yes always, delighted when they discover who they are and what they were meant to contribute to the world. It will be the greatest secret you will ever know and it won't be hidden in some shadowy, dark place.

In the light of your life plan:

- You will discover that you are unique and connected to everyone else at the same time.

- You will discover that you are not only good, but also intended to be great in specific ways.

- You will discover that you have special gifts that come easily, even naturally, and require no training or experience in order to use them effectively.

- You will discover that your piece of the life puzzle is the only one like it, with a special shape and openings and extensions that perfectly connect with the pieces of every other person's piece in the puzzle.

- You will discover that you have the potential to make a profound difference in the world, where you are right now and possibly everywhere later.

- You will discover that you were intended to live your life each day in joy and through love, and share your joy and love with everyone you meet.

No one is void of a powerful plan. Euripides, the Greek playwright (480–406 BC), made that clear centuries ago, "There is but one life for each of us: our own." When you are true to who you were intended to be, you are fully supported by the source of your plan.

All life plans come with a *Promise* or guarantee. This *Promise* is directly tied to knowing and following your life plan. The *Promise* is given to everyone equally and with the same intention, which is for people to joyfully and lovingly serve one another.

A promise is given that if you will follow your life plan and listen to your personal wisdom in the service of others, you will be provided the experiences, relationships, and resources to live a life filled with joy and love.

Using your life plan and fulfilling the *Promise* honors your potential and the potential of every other person in the world. When you place your piece into the puzzle, as introduced at the beginning of this book, we will all be the beneficiaries of *your* potential to support *our* potential. Your life plan is your compass to guide the best and right choices and purposeful actions. Your plan is the source of your power to influence the world, transform situations, and change lives, all by just being yourself.

The power of the *Promise* attracts the matching people, opportunities, situations, and even things. When you love, you will attract love. When you support others, you will be supported. When you share your life plan with the world through your daily choices, you will have health, wealth, and everything needed to be who you are. This is called the Law of Attraction and it is one of the major laws of the Universe.

Basically, it says like attracts like. Live your life plan and you will easily attract all that is necessary for you to succeed. But the Law of Attraction also applies to the opposite of your life plan. Get away from your plan by living your life to acquire or possess things, take advantage of people, or be a person you were not intended to be, and you will get what matches that, too. You will find yourself struggling and faced with difficulties and scarcity. Remember, in the Law of Attraction, like attracts like.

Look at your life now and ask yourself what you have attracted in your relationships, work, health, and experiences. You have attracted what matches who you have been and what you have been doing. Follow your life plan; use it as a compass to direct your choices and you will attract what brings you joy and love.

It is up to you, and you hold in your hand the tool and the process to show you what and how. Isn't it time to know the truth about you?

Your Path to Joy with Love

Before you begin the process to explore and discover your life plan, the purpose of your plan must be clear. This is not a plan you must follow to avoid punishment or within which you have no choices to make. It is definitely not a plan with points along the way, like a goal plan. Most importantly, your life plan is not your destiny; it is your potential. Whether you fully experience that potential will be up to you and the choices you make from an endless field of possibilities that are constantly presenting themselves to you. These possibilities fill every moment of your life and always have.

In each moment you have had the power to choose, and what you chose determined what happened next, including the field of possibilities that would be presented next. That is where the power of each human being exists, in the choices from the field of possibilities they make in each moment of their lives.

Unfortunately, most people limit their potential by focusing on only a few possibilities and choosing from those. We set up endless moments of "either or" choices, often choosing between something we don't desire and something even worse. This is where people feel they have no choices, as they continue to choose negative and disempowering possibilities, with the inevitable consequences that match those choices. Life appears hopeless and people feel helpless. When the field of possibilities is limited in this way, people end up living what Henry David Thoreau called, ". . . lives of quiet desperation."

The truth is that you, like everyone else, have always had and still have endless possible choices. You just don't see them or look for them. When you know your life plan, you will see many more possibilities, even endless possibilities, available in every moment for you to live your life plan and do so with a powerful purpose.

The purpose of your life plan is to guide you to live each day from and in joy and to share your joy through love with other people. So you will be choosing from the possible choices that create joy and come from love. Your life plan is the best and right path to joy for you, and a life of love while supporting the joy of others.

You will use your plan as the compass to guide your choices to live, work, and have relationships that are grounded in love. You will give love to your activities, interactions, and work, without questioning what you should or must do—you will know what to do. That means serving other people and the world without fear and judgment. As idealistic as that may sound, it is the easiest and only way to fulfilling joy. Your life plan is your path there.

Love is not necessarily romantic or about a relationship with another person. Love is wider and deeper than an experience or a relationship. Love is a spiritual connection, the heart connection we can make to anything, including people. People can love their work, a cause, a purpose, a pet, nature, blue skies, etc.

It is not important what or who we love, or how we love and connect to it or them. This connected love doesn't seek to possess, need, or have. This love honors connection, desires the best, and allows things and others to be what and who they are without judgment or attempting to change them. First and foremost, pure love honors ourselves and allows us to make mistakes and learn from them. Such love begins with who we are, our personal life plan, and our potential experiences on the path following our plan.

When you begin to live and choose from your plan, you will know and experience this love without expectations or limits, and you will know joy and manifest that joy in all you do and whatever you experience.

Joy is something we seek and often never know. Yes, we tell people to be happy, and often they are happy and so are we. But happiness is only a temporary contentment or satisfaction with what we are doing, what is happening, or who we are with. It is fleeting, and when situations change, it changes too.

Interestingly, we have been taught to find happiness as if it were a one-time experience resulting from a lifelong pursuit. No wonder so many people are unhappy. They are pursuing a temporary and fleeting state rather than the expanding and permanent state of joy.

Real joy is the awareness and recognition of our connections. We can experience joy in a sunrise, a loving whisper, or an act of kindness. Joy is both a feeling and an experience marked by balance, alignment, and acceptance. Joy is intended to define the moments of our relationships, work, and lives. Nothing is more powerful or attractive.

When you follow your life plan and focus on choosing what brings love and joy, you will be blessed with passion. Passion is like gasoline; it fuels your desires and motivates your actions. Living on the path of your life plan will guarantee you never lack passion. Passion is so powerful that when you are experiencing it, time and fatigue do not exist.

Inspiration and intuition will arise from your passion and will further enlighten your path by showing you the endless field of possibilities. Your passion will attract more opportunities to express and share as the world opens up to fulfill your desires, wishes, and dreams.

The plan is the path for never-ending love and joy fueled by passion. Love, passion, and joy are life itself. To know and experience them, you will have to know and follow your life plan, using it as your compass to choose your path each day. You will feel fully alive, as Howard Thurman invited you to do when he said, "Don't ask what the world needs. Ask what makes you come alive and then go and do it, because what the world needs is people who have come alive."

So you can see that the plan is important, vitally important, and it is time for you to discover your plan and your path. A gentle reminder before we get started discovering your plan: it is important to follow *The Guide* as it is written. The plan reveals itself like a beautiful flower—one petal at a time. Don't try to rush your beautiful flower. Let it reveal itself to you as you are ready to know and understand it. Let's get started.

The Components of *Your* Life Plan

 Your life plan is comprised of six components. The content of any one of the components will not be unique to you, and may in fact be the same content of a component found in another person's life plan. However, when the six components come together as your plan, the totality of the plan will be unique to you. No two life plans are exactly the same! That makes your life plan sacred and powerful. If you are not following your plan, the potential effects on you and the world are lost.

The Guide will help you explore and discover what is contained in each of your plan's six components. You will also discover the important relationship between the components and how they flow together and in and out of each other to create your impact on the world.

And you will begin to experience the love and joy these components can open to you.

Each component has its own power and has been affecting your life since the day you were born. Put them together (as you will here), and the plan reveals a path to follow, choices to make, and experiences to create. The profound power and influence of your plan and the components making up that plan over a lifetime cannot be overstated.

As you begin to consider the components of your life plan, you will recognize some familiar terms. In society the words vision, purpose, and mission are often used interchangeably. In this process they are very different things. So you are asked to set aside what you were taught or believed a vision, purpose, or mission to be, and how you may have thought of these terms in your own life. This is also true of gifts, standards, and needs.

By the time you complete your life plan, you will know their differences and how those differences create the flow of your life plan. Let's begin to get a sense of how the terms are used in *The Guide* and how they are defined in your life plan. Note the specificity of each component as you start to see the relationships they have to each other.

The first component in your life plan is your *personal life vision.* This vision represents a view of what is most important in life. It is a message you are asked to share with the world. Many people may have the same life vision or variations of the same one, making this component the most similar one from plan to plan. Yet, a life vision is very personal and can't be found or designed; a life vision is discovered. You have had glimpses of your life vision throughout your life, but probably didn't recognize or fully see it, but you will.

The second component of your life plan is your *personal life purpose.* This purpose is your specific and unique expression of your life vision. The expression of your purpose is how you live and interact with the world each day. Your life purpose will be the "real you." People with similar or even the same life visions can have very different life purposes.

The third component of your life plan is your *personal life mission.* Your mission is the action part of your life plan. It is what you will *do* to express your life purpose and share your vision. Your mission will be the activities, work, and experiences where you are being the "real you." The combination of your life purpose and mission is very specific to you.

The tools you will use to share your vision with the world are the fourth component of your life plan. Your *personal gifts* are how you express your purpose and do (actions) your mission. Gifts provide you a special way of seeing, knowing, and doing.

As a plan component, you will use your gifts to follow your life plan and make daily choices on your path of love and joy. Your gifts are invaluable and often hard to describe to other people. You probably don't know how they work when you are using them or how easily they have led to skill development and mastery in the past.

Some people would call them talents, but they are much more. They are also the key to your life plan because they are the unique tools that make your life plan a reality. Knowing and using your gifts will make everything easier, and when you are using them you will do it lovingly and joyfully.

The fifth component of your life plan is your *standards,* or the guides for your daily choices. These are like values, but not the values society talks about. You are born with these standards; you don't learn them as you do values and beliefs. Think of standards as where you will stand to use your gifts, pursue your mission, express your purpose, and share your vision.

The last life plan component, which is actually the default component of your plan, is your *ego-mind.* It sounds quite different than the other five components, because it is. It is the component that substitutes for the other components when necessary. This component can produce both positive and negative results and even thwart your life plan, especially when you don't know your plan or have allowed external influences to pull you away from living your intended plan. The ego-mind uses egoic needs as the tools to direct your choices when you are being guided by your ego-mind.

Since the majority of people don't know the plan for their lives, the ego-mind is directing their lives and the choices they are making each day. The worst result is that most human behavior originates in egoic needs and hinders the behavior that would originate from standards. Choosing from needs rather than standards totally changes our life experiences and is the root cause of unhappiness, dissatisfaction, and stress. However, the awareness you will have as you complete *The Guide* will help you recognize how to fulfill your egoic needs in order to rely more on your standards to make loving and joyful choices.

The ego-mind and egoic needs can become a positively powerful part of living your life plan. They can become an advocate for your plan by prompting you to follow your plan to guide your choices. That will happen when your ego-mind and egoic needs are no longer unconsciously acting as the default for your intended life plan. They then join the plan and provide useful guidance, even though they are ready to fill in if needed.

As you proceed through *The Guide*, you will explore and discover your life plan through these six components. As you put the components together, you will also recognize the interdependence of them. It is the seamless contribution of each component to the whole plan that provides the guidance for your life, work, and relationships.

From your plan, your life will consist of powerful choices that navigate a path of adventure, joy, and connections to the life plans of others. As a result, your piece of the life puzzle will be gently guided into its intended place with love and joy. With your piece of the puzzle in place, your life will be a powerful part of the message of the puzzle to the world, which is that we are all intended to experience and share pure love and pure joy throughout our lives, within our relationships, and through our work. That is the purpose of your plan, my plan, and every plan; it is the purpose of life itself.

Your Personal Life Vision

Your personal life vision is the foundation for all you will discover in *The Guide* about your life plan. It will provide insight into a lot of what has happened in your life experiences and why they felt the way they did at the time, and especially later. As you move through this section and later sections of *The Guide*, your vision will continue to reveal itself, often in surprising ways.

The vision you begin discovering in this section may not be the one you end up with when you complete *The Guide*. That is part of the process of clarity found as the components of your life plan are revealed, especially their relationship to each other.

Think of your personal vision as the big picture you envision for the world. Your life vision is your sense of what matters most in life and what is possible for you and other people. It is what you want the world to know about experiencing love and joy. Your vision will inspire the best in people because it is about the best in people.

Your personal life vision is also the foundation for the real you and what you were meant to do with your life. However, and this is important, your life vision will not be about you individually, even though you will discover it through your own experiences.

A life vision is a statement of what is necessary and possible for all human beings to experience joy and live in love.

A life vision is general and even vague by definition, yet it is powerful enough to change the world! Let's begin exploring your personal life vision by having you answer the following questions:

If you knew you were going to die tomorrow and could tell the world the most important thing you know about life, what would you say?

The world would be a better place if people . . .

About themselves, I wish people knew that...

From your answers you can see that a vision is an opportunity to be a visionary about life. You can also see that your personal vision is closely related to your personal experiences, including big changes and crises that have occurred, as well as achievements and even tragedies that have affected you. All of these experiences and situations can help reveal your vision. Your vision is not the cause of what happened to you, but what happened offers valuable insights and glimpses of what is profound and meaningful to you.

Therefore, life experience can make it easier to identify and clarify your life vision, but only if you are willing to be reflective and introspective without regret and judgment. Life experiences can also cloud your life vision and the other components of your life plan if you get attached to the feelings, pain, or even the rewards of those experiences. Consider your life experiences as revealing the components of your life plan.

For your vision, you are looking for a recurring theme from your experiences. Remember the life puzzle metaphor mentioned earlier that identified you as a piece of the puzzle into which everyone fits? Think of your vision as one of the themes or messages for the entire puzzle that you can discover through examining your personal experiences. Write the theme you are thinking of below, using the previous questions and provided ideas:

My life vision is . . .

Go ahead and play with the words and create a single succinct sentence below. Remember, your vision is a global statement; it isn't specific to you, and many others may have the same or similar vision.

My life vision is . . .

Let's see how you did. What follows are three actual life plans which will be used throughout *The Guide* to illustrate how the components of a life plan come together and guide daily living. Do not copy the examples into your plan or attempt to make your plan fit the examples. It won't work due to the unique nature of every life plan, including yours.

Also, note that the life experiences of each person were part of the discovery and exploration of their life plan. Their experiences did not define their plan (it may appear that way), but helped them to see what resonated with them and what did not. The more life experience you have, the clearer your plan will become, too.

There is one caution about your previous experiences and the experiences you see here. When people start following this process, it is tempting to try to fit their experiences, training, and résumés into their plans. That is useful information, so do keep it in mind to provide clues to your plan. Just know that you may end up doing some of what you did in the past, but then again you may not, or you may do it differently when you know your plan.

As you work your way through The Guide, the process will again use these three examples to illustrate a particular plan component. So, we begin with a brief overview of each person's life and application of their life plan, and then their vision is presented. See if your vision has the same power and potential.

Jane M. (*The Guide* author)

Jane began her career as a teacher and athletic coach. Over time, her interest in the human mind, behavior, and success led to a career in sport psychology and eventually life coaching. In her thirty-six years of working with people who wanted to be successful and happy, she discovered that people did not know and therefore didn't trust their potential and capabilities. The people who were confident had a vision of what was possible for them and thrived with the challenges of living. Those who didn't know the powerful possibilities for their lives struggled to survive and find success. Today she continues in life coaching and sport psychology, but focuses her work and life on helping people to know and trust their potential and their possibilities.

Jane's vision is: Everyone is born with a magnificent potential and has full access to a field of possibilities to experience and share their potential.

Bob R.

Bob left an earlier career in sales to be a stay-at-home dad for his three children, while his wife held a corporate management position. As the children became fully engaged in school and outside activities, Bob decided he was ready to return to working full-time. From his previous experiences and especially his daily experiences with his children, he knew he wanted to contribute to the world in ways that helped people thrive and live with passion. He longed for balance and more freedom to live each day with integrity in all aspects of his life, work, and relationships. Bob currently oversees a foundation for single and newly married parents of young children. He is also active in community recreation programs as a coach and mentor.

Bob's vision is: Each day is a new opportunity to create loving connections to what is most important in life.

Kate C.

Kate was a corporate attorney for ten years. During that time she also volunteered with a women's professional association to teach girls about starting their own businesses. While she enjoyed the relationships in her work, she realized that she enjoyed preparing and teaching the groups of girls even more. She noticed that she was more joyful and playful and that the girls glowed as they learned how they could succeed in the business world. She also noticed that she often came home from her corporate position drained and frustrated by the expectations and stress of meeting deadlines. She was ready to live her life plan more fully, but was concerned about income and not knowing what to do. Today Kate travels the world setting up and managing unique conferences for girls and women who want to own their own businesses. These conferences include workshops, materials, and networking in which she also participates.

Kate's vision is: People can be happy and successful only when they pursue and live their dreams.

After considering the examples and reviewing what you wrote, rewrite your vision statement below. Later, as you complete each of the life plan components you will continue revisiting your life vision for updating and clarity.

My life vision is:

When you are somewhat comfortable with your life vision statement, you will be ready to start exploring your life purpose. Don't get stuck here looking for the perfect statement or words. This is just a beginning and you will be revisiting your vision statement as you discover the other components. So let's move on and see how your life purpose flows out of your personal vision and provides the path for sharing your vision with the world.

Your Personal Life Purpose

Often when people talk about life purpose, they refer to vision, purpose, and mission as different words for the same thing. These three words have an interdependent relationship, but they do not mean the same thing. As you discover your life purpose, you will find that your purpose flows from your vision, and that flow defines their relationship.

When you are living your life purpose, you serve others and that service illuminates your vision for them. You could think of passionately living your life purpose as an act of true love. Whereas your life vision is generally not about you, your purpose is very much about you.

*A life purpose is the unique personal expression of your vision for the world. It is who you are **being** for the world to experience your vision.*

People will know you by your life purpose and will love how your purpose impacts them. Knowing your purpose is not knowing what to do, but knowing who to be! It is you, "being you." You will be the most loving and kind when you are being yourself. It will give meaning to your life and it will be the meaning that matters most.

Being and living your life purpose will be marked by passion. This is not the passion of needs and wants, nor the passion of frenetic energy, obsession, and irresponsibility. Your purpose will stimulate a passion marked by love and presence with devotion, not to outcomes, but to who you are being. Passion arising out of purpose is energy enhancing, even contagious, and always inspiring.

You will live your purpose not because you should, have to, or others want you to. You will live your purpose because of your passion, whether or not others like it or even accept who you are being or what you are doing from it. Your passion will be obvious in what you are doing and who you are being, not in your thoughts or plans. When you know your purpose, it will not leave you alone, calling you to passionately live and share your vision with the world.

It is important here to note the difference between passion and ego-driven anxiety. Passion is a present state of expressing a purpose and using gifts, not a result of doing something. The passion happens within the experience; it is not the reason for the experience or for doing something.

Ego-driven anxiety can look like passion, but is an emotional state that occurs before doing something or after doing it. This anxiety is common in anything that causes stress responses, is difficult to do, or requires you to keep learning more skills. Something chosen from anxiety or to prevent anxiety is probably not connected to your purpose. Stress, struggle, and working at something all come from your ego-mind pressing to fulfill a need to achieve or possess something.

Most importantly, if you feel a lot of internal resistance, usually evidenced by procrastination and avoidance, you are moving or choosing away from your purpose. Choosing from ego or off-purpose is most evident in careers or jobs. Many people spend most of their working days in jobs that keep them from their life purpose. They don't know their life plan and are seduced by cultural expectations of working for money and status. Society even tells us that making money and what we dream of being and doing are mutually exclusive—they are not. Our life dreams, especially recurring ones, are glimpses of our life plans calling to us.

It is sad to see so many people who know there is something more powerful and passionate intended for them, but who have given up on their dreams. If dreams can't be immediately seen as leading to money and status, the dreams are criticized as unrealistic or impractical. The irony of these glimpses of our life plans is that if we were to follow our dreams, the money, resources, and people to support our success would come at the right time and in the right way for us to passionately share our life vision with the world. This is the *Promise* discussed at the beginning of this book. That comes with your life plan and your dreams to guarantee your success and joy.

Finally, not doing work or having a career that expresses your personal purpose and life vision is the biggest threat to your health and happiness. Your life plan is the guide to the intended path for your life, not just your work and career. Your health and happiness are the result of living a purposeful life. That purpose will enhance your relationships and turn each day into a wonderful, passionate adventure. Less stress means better health and balance, too.

A life purpose lived is a gift to yourself and to all the people in your life. So let's get to your life purpose, where the passion to fully support your health, happiness, and wealth is waiting for you to capture it.

To discover your life purpose, you are going to have to play with words, thoughts, and feelings. You will probably come up with a number of versions before the clarity comes. Even when you think you know your purpose, you will have to test it in your experiences. The feedback from those experiences will help you focus your purpose even more while increasing your passion to live it. Eventually you will only have to tweak it from time to time as you see the details of following your passion and expressing your purpose through your life.

Let's begin the discovery of your life purpose by revisiting your life vision.

My life vision is . . .

Now read the vision to yourself a couple of times. Read the following question and then close your eyes to visualize possible answers. Record your answers and go on.

If you were doing something that expressed your vision to others without you telling them that vision, what would you be doing?

To add to your possibilities, consider your life purpose as an experience. Read the question again, close your eyes, consider possibilities for each of the following questions, and then write your answers under each question.

If you were "being and doing" your life purpose (without knowing it right now), what would the experience feel and look like for you?

If you were "being and doing" your life purpose, what would the experience feel and look like for other people who are interacting with you?

Lastly, reflect on your experiences with other people or when you were doing something for them, particularly the experiences that were easy, effortless, passionate (not frenetic), and enjoyable. Close your eyes and visualize each of the following situations. Record your answers for each situation before going on to the next one.

What was the environment or setting that most supported who you were being and what you were doing in the service of others?

Who was involved in the experiences? Were they children, adults, family, special groups, or people in need of something you had to offer? List them and any characteristics unique to them.

Finally, what were you doing exactly? For example, were you talking, making something, putting something together, helping others figure something out, etc.?

Discovering a life purpose is a series of approximations (what it could be), and eliminations (what it isn't). Look back at your answers to the previous questions and answer the following questions:

Think about a situation you enjoyed and felt passionate about your participation or actions. It was probably easy to do and didn't require too much thinking or planning for you to do it well and have others benefit. What were you doing and for whom?

What situations, people, and activities caused stress and anxiety, and left you drained?

You have answered a lot of questions and probably have some valuable answers. Let's get to the writing of your first life purpose statement with the information you have discovered. It is helpful to have your life vision statement in front of you as you do this, so write it again here:

My life vision is . . .

You are going to write your life purpose using three parts that you will combine in a single sentence. You will be looking for:

- Who you will share your vision with or who you will serve.
- What you will experience or do for others and who you will be in that experience.

- What other people will experience through your vision and your purposeful actions.

Based on what you know so far from the previous questions and the review of your life vision, fill in the following spaces that correspond to the three parts above:

- The people or group of people who would most benefit from knowing your life vision.

- What it will feel like for you to share your vision with the people you identified above.

- How other people will know your vision and how their experiences and lives could change.

Write a life purpose statement below based on what you have written above and before. You will write a few versions before we are done, so be open and playful in writing a one-sentence statement with the three parts above included. This is not easy and can be cumbersome at first. You will get clarity as we go.

My life purpose is:

Let's now check back with the three previous life plan examples of Jane, Bob, and Kate to see how a purpose statement looks and sounds. Look for the three parts of a purpose statement you considered above. The examples provide a context for each of the individuals' life purpose and vision for their life path.

Later we won't include all of the biographical information, but for now it is still helpful. Make special note of how the purpose is different from the vision, yet flows out of it. A life purpose is the personal expression of a life vision or who the person is being.

Jane M.

Jane began her career as a teacher and athletic coach. Over time, her interest in the human mind, behavior, and success led to a career in sport psychology and eventually life coaching. In her thirty-six years of working with people who wanted to be successful and happy, she discovered that people did not know and therefore didn't trust their potential and capabilities. The people who were confident had a vision of what was possible for them and thrived with life's challenges. Those who didn't know the powerful possibilities for their lives struggled to survive and find success. Today she continues in life coaching and sport psychology, but focuses her life and work on helping people to know and trust their potential and their possibilities.

Jane's vision is: Everyone is born with a magnificent potential and has full access to a field of possibilities to experience and share their potential.

Jane's purpose is: To guide and inspire people to know and live their potential and possibilities.

Bob R.

Bob left an earlier career in sales to be a stay-at-home dad for his three children, while his wife held a corporate management position. As the children became fully engaged in school and outside activities, Bob decided he was ready to return to working full-time. From his previous experiences and especially his daily experiences with his children, he knew he wanted to contribute to the world in ways that helped people thrive and live with passion. He longed for balance and more freedom to live each day with integrity in all aspects of his life, work, and relationships. Bob currently oversees a foundation for single and newly married parents of young children. He is also active in community recreation programs as a coach and mentor.

Bob's vision is: Each day is a new opportunity to create loving connections to what is most important in life.

Bob's purpose is: To make it easier for people to have loving connections to what and who are most important to them.

Kate C.

Kate was a corporate attorney for ten years. During that time she also volunteered with a women's professional association to teach girls about starting their own businesses. While she enjoyed the relationships in her work, she realized that she enjoyed preparing and teaching the groups of girls even more. She noticed that she was more joyful and playful and that the girls glowed as they learned how they could succeed in the business world. She also noticed that she often came home from her corporate position drained and frustrated by the expectations and stress of meeting deadlines. She was ready to live her life plan more fully, but was concerned about income and not knowing what to do. Today Kate travels the world setting up and managing unique conferences for girls and women who want to own their own businesses. These conferences include workshops, materials, and networking in which she also participates.

Kate's vision is: People can be happy and successful only when they pursue and live their dreams.

Kate's purpose is: To bring together people, materials, and support so people can experience and live their dreams.

You are ready to write your purpose statement again. After reading the above examples, go back and review your vision statement as well as the answers you wrote to the questions, your experience, and the experiences of others above. Write what you think your purpose statement could be now.

My life purpose is . . .

Read your purpose statement out loud and pay attention to how it sounds and feels. Does it sound powerful? Is it clear and passionate? Does the statement start you thinking of how you have previously acted from your life purpose or could act now? Tinker with the words and write it again.

My life purpose is . . .

You were asked earlier to think about your previous positive experiences that were easy, passionate, and energetic. Read your written purpose statement. Does it match the earlier experiences you considered to be easy, passionate, and energetic? How does it feel and how deeply do you feel it? A life purpose is the source of authentic power and passion and it will feel that way—does yours?

This is a good point to introduce you to an essential resource for exploring your life plan—a *Thesaurus*. You will be referring to it often throughout *The Guide*, so if you don't own one, please buy or borrow one now. It will be a valuable resource and may be your key to knowing your life plan. Once you have a *Thesaurus*, go on.

In the *Thesaurus*, look up the action words you have been using for your vision and purpose statements. As you read the alternative words the *Thesaurus* suggests for your current words, look for other possible words that feel like a better fit for you. These words may jump off the page and resonate with you as an emotional reaction or even a tingling sensation in your body. If none of the words affects you, you may already have the best word. If you find something you like, plug it into your vision or purpose statement and check the power and passion again.

Language is important and words matter. Hidden within them are clues in the form of how they feel and what they inspire within us. Words are also limiting in that sometimes they cannot adequately portray the power and passion we want or feel.

Do the best you can with them, but be patient and take your time to find the best words. The more time you take with it now, the easier the next four components of your life plan will be to discover. The vision and purpose statements are important, so you want to have them as accurate as possible before you continue.

Finally, there is one other important tool to help you with the words and phrasing of your life purpose. People you know, or even acquaintances have been reflecting your vision and purpose back to you throughout your life. Other people often experience our life plan before we know it. We will discuss this in more detail later when we talk about your personal gifts.

For now, take a few moments and reflect on what people have told you, written about you, or told others about you. Of course, we are looking for the positive things, not the criticisms or judgments. The most helpful descriptions of you will center on who you have been or what you have done that affected and inspired others. Reflect on what you recall from job evaluations, personal praise, letters, e-mails, or comments and conversations.

List below the words, phrases, or compliments that stand out:

Now review your last written life purpose and look at the list above. Are there some words, phrases, or behaviors that others have provided which make a better fit for your life purpose and life vision? If so, plug them in. You may have to consult your *Thesaurus* again, too. Rewrite your life vision and life purpose below. When you are satisfied with them, move on to the next section on life mission.

My life vision is:

My life purpose is:

Your Personal Life Mission

Discovering and clarifying your life mission is challenging, but without knowing your life plan, it can seem impossible. This is the "What should I be doing?" question people typically want answered when they pick up this book or others like it. People want to know the work, career, and environment that will make them happy. They are often frustrated and drained by what they are currently doing, knowing it can't or won't make them happy. When work consumes so much time in our lives, it should bring us joy and we should love doing it.

The "doing" question can't be answered without knowing the purpose for our doing. Thus, knowing your life vision and purpose before exploring what you should be "doing," is necessary. If you have completed the first two components in *The Guide*, you should already know your vision and purpose and be ready to know what to do from them. If you haven't completed those components, please go back and do them before proceeding with the exploration of your mission.

We live in a society that continually reminds us that success and wealth will be determined by what we do. Our schools begin early in the educational process to steer children's, and eventually adult's choices toward what they can do to make money in order to acquire things. Are the house, the car, the retirement accounts, the family, and other things important? Of course they are, but they can be very costly if acquiring them requires you to abandon the purpose of your life.

The work you do each day and over a career cannot be different from what was intended for you. If it is, you miss much of the passion and joy intended for your daily experiences, interactions with others, and work experiences. Tragically, people can spend a lifetime working outside their vision, purpose, and mission, with their gifts dormant. People are often aware that this is happening to them when they describe the feeling of a vague "something else" pulling them in a different direction. Many people wait for their retirement years to finally do what they describe as, "What I always wanted to do." When you know your life plan and the path for your life, you won't have to wait for your retirement.

The disconnection between who we are and what we do is also evident in our beliefs about "doing." A major fear, again perpetuated by society, is that if people were to do what they wanted to do, it would not provide the money for them to have what they need to be happy. Being happy in what we are doing doesn't mean sacrificing wealth, abundance, and enjoyment.

When you share your vision, live your purpose, and do your mission using your gifts, abundance will flow to you easily and effortlessly. Why would you be given a life plan with the tools to follow that plan, if what was needed to be successful wasn't going to be provided? It is and will be provided if you trust your life plan and take the path it directs you to follow.

A life mission is what you do to express your purpose, share your vision, and use your gifts.

People experience your vision for themselves through what you do for and with them.

Your mission statement will be longer than your life vision or life purpose. Where the vision and purpose statements were one sentence each, your mission will consist of three or four statements of areas of "doing." It is centered in activities, actions, tasks, and programs or projects. It is also quite skills-oriented. These skills are easily learned because you have the gifts to master the skills (more on this later.) Your mission will be what you do and how you do it, to live your purpose and share your vision.

To know what you should do as your life mission, it is easier to know first what you may be doing that isn't your life mission. When you are attached to the outcomes of what you are doing and how you do it, whether in work, relationships, or life, it may not be your mission. Attachment is marked by being heavily invested in the approval and acceptance of others. You may even seek their permission and reassuring support for your efforts and your motives. You feel drained and overwhelmed, and often don't like what you are doing.

A big clue that you are not doing your mission is that you live for Fridays and dread Mondays. The attachment, struggle with, and resistance to what you are doing may seem normal in our society, but these are actually symptoms of being off your mission and being driven by your ego. (Again, more on this later.)

How can you know if what you are doing is aligned with your life mission? When you are "doing" your life mission, you will do what you do with ease and passion. It won't be a question of what or how to do it, only a question of where and with whom you do it. Your life mission is the experience intersection of your purpose and the world in which you live. When these elements intersect, the experience works for you and it works for the world. This has an entirely different feel from "doing" outside your mission.

"Doing," arising from your mission, feels inspiring and energizing. "Doing" outside your mission or from your ego, feels like obligations and have-to's. Stop for a moment and think about what you have been doing recently, especially career-wise. Are you doing what you're doing for money, because you are trained to do it, or because you just don't know what else to do? Let's find out what your life plan says you should be doing with your skills, time, and energy. Begin by reviewing your vision and purpose. Transfer them below.

My life vision is . . .

My life purpose is . . .

Look at your vision and purpose for a few moments. Close your eyes and imagine what you would be doing today to serve other people if you were living the vision and expressing the purpose in your life and work. List those experiences or actions below. Please don't censor any of them as impossible or omit any that you are not trained or prepared to do. List them all.

Review what you have written. Close your eyes and imagine that there is more you could do from your vision and purpose than you had thought. Let yourself dream big here. Write those experiences or activities here.

Look back over your imagined "doings" and circle the words, phrases, tasks, or situations that reoccur and resonate with you, meaning they emotionally connect with you. Write them here.

With these experiences, activities, or actions in mind, you are going to do some exploring or fieldwork outside of you. For the next couple of days, observe the work, situations, or tasks other people are engaged in, especially those who seem happy doing what they do and those that are passionate about it. Record your observations below as the label or title for what they were doing and exactly what they did.

| Label or Title | What They Do |

A common mistake people make when they are looking to do something different, especially in their work or career, is to identify with the label or title of what someone does. For example, attorneys who want to change careers often say they want to become teachers. They think about what their favorite teachers did and see themselves doing the same. However, lots of people "do" very similar work, but are not teachers. For example, river guides, life coaches, and national park interpreters also teach, but in different environments. What they do is actually the most appealing thing about teaching—they connect people to new information or skills and show them how to use what they've learned to enjoy life or an experience more.

That is what many of the attorneys thought they would do with the law and their clients. Unfortunately, they often found themselves in an adversarial system where winning and generating income, not connecting people to information, dominated the process. So it wasn't that they wanted to be teachers; they wanted to experience (do) what they perceived teachers experience (do).

Look back at what you observed other people doing. Also, look at the labels and titles and consider who else might do those same things. Write your discoveries below.

Titles and labels of people who do similar things:

What other people do that I could see myself doing, which would allow me to share my vision and act from my purpose:

Now look at the three evolving life plans of Jane, Bob, and Kate from the previous discussions of vision and purpose. Again, the information is included for each individual to allow the identification of vision, purpose, and now mission in their life choices. Please note the length of the mission statements and the differences in how their mission was identified and flowed from their vision and purpose.

Jane M.

Jane began her career as a teacher and athletic coach. Over time, her interest in the human mind, behavior, and success led to a career in sport psychology and eventually life coaching. In her thirty-six years of working with people who wanted to be successful and happy, she discovered that people did not know and therefore didn't trust their potential and capabilities. The people who were confident had a vision of what was possible for them and thrived with life's challenges. Those who didn't know the powerful possibilities for their lives struggled to survive and find success. Today she continues in life coaching and sport psychology, but focuses her life and work on helping people to know and trust their potential and their possibilities.

Jane's vision is: Everyone is born with a magnificent potential and has full access to a field of possibilities to experience and share their potential.

Jane's purpose is: To guide and inspire people to know and live their potential and possibilities.

Jane's mission is:

1. To provide sensible and usable information and strategies for people to see and easily experience their potential.

2. To design and create programs and materials to help people experience the possibilities that can inspire them.

3. To supply the guidance and support to people who are willing to explore and discover their potential.

Bob R.

Bob left an earlier career in sales to be a stay-at-home dad for his three children, while his wife held a corporate management position. As the children became fully engaged in school and outside activities, Bob decided he was ready to return to working full-time. From his previous experiences and especially his daily experiences with his children, he knew he wanted to contribute to the world in ways that helped people thrive and live with passion. He longed for balance and more freedom to live each day with integrity in all aspects of his life, work, and relationships. Bob currently oversees a foundation for single and newly married parents of young children. He is also active in community recreation programs as a coach and mentor.

Bob's vision is: Each day is a new opportunity to create loving connections to what is most important in life.

Bob's purpose is: To make it easier for people to have loving connections to what and who are most important to them.

Bob's mission is:

1. To support and participate in groups that easily connect people to what they love.
2. To encourage people to connect to each other with love and kindness.
3. To design and present materials and programs for parents to honor what is most important through their connections.

Kate C.

Kate was a corporate attorney for ten years. During that time she also volunteered with a women's professional association to teach girls about starting their own businesses. While she enjoyed the relationships in her work, she realized that she enjoyed preparing and teaching the groups of girls even more. She noticed that she was more joyful and playful and that the girls glowed as they learned how they could succeed in the business world. She also noticed that she often came home from her corporate position drained and frustrated by the expectations and stress of meeting deadlines. She was ready to live her life plan more fully, but was concerned about income and not knowing what to do. Today Kate travels the world setting up and managing unique conferences for girls and women who want to own their own businesses. These conferences include workshops, materials, and networking in which she also participates.

Kate's vision is: People can be happy and successful only when they pursue and live their dreams.

Kate's purpose is: To bring together people, materials, and support so people can experience and live their dreams.

Kate's mission is:

1. To bring the strengths and wisdom of people together.

2. To provide experiences for instant success, on which confidence can be built.

3. To share knowledge and strategies for people to know their dreams and live them.

Let's review your life plan and what you have observed and identified for your mission. Using the examples above, write your life mission statement. Complete the information below.

My life vision is . . .

My purpose is to . . .

What I see myself doing and in what situations . . .

Possible mission statements (emphasize what you will do):

My mission is . . .

1.

2.

3.

Now close your eyes and see yourself experiencing your mission as you have stated it above. Remember, this is what you are doing. Any insights? *Rewrite the mission statements below.*

My mission is . . .

1.

2.

3.

The mission statement is the component that will challenge you the most as you explore your life plan. Fortunately, the other components, when clarified, will also help to clarify your mission. So you will be returning to this component many times over the upcoming years.

Be patient, it will reveal itself—usually slowly, as you do your currently known mission and fine-tune it. You will also definitely be finding out what your mission isn't, based on what is difficult, frustrating, and does not allow you to express your purpose and use your gifts.

It is time to check the connection and flow of your plan so far. Remember, it all begins with your life vision, a view that you would like the world to know and experience. That is followed by your life purpose, which is your personal expression of that vision. Finally, your mission is what you will do to share the vision and express your purpose.

A vision flows down to the purpose, which flows down to the mission. It is like a funnel of specificity that goes from the general at the top (vision) to the uniquely specific at the bottom (mission), with the purpose in between.

Write your components below and see if they flow down from one to the next. You may want to share them with someone who can ask you questions or give you feedback to further clarify the specificity and flow of your life plan components.

My life vision is . . .

My purpose is . . .

My mission is . . .

1.

2.

3.

It is recommended that you now take the three components you have so far and write them on a 3x5" index card. Carry this card with you and from time to time, take it out and read it aloud. The power of this card will be explained later in detail when we discuss how the entire life plan will fit on a 3x5" card. For now, know that when you read this card, you are asking an important question, "What are my life vision, purpose, and mission?"

You will notice words, phrases, songs, things other people say, or things you read, answering this question by leading you back to what you have discovered so far and providing more direction and clues. This can be quite a magical process, with insights and illuminations almost daily. It is important that you don't dismiss anything that resonates with you or hooks your attention at this time. If something shows up and grabs you, make note of it in the back of this book and you will get a chance to use it later in *The Guide*.

Your Personal Gifts

You are now ready to discover and explore one of the most fulfilling and unique components of your life plan, your personal gifts. We have been laying a foundation for your gifts with the discovery of your vision, purpose, and mission. Now it is time to discover those unique tools in your life plan that make it easy to live your vision, purpose, and mission.

Your personal gifts can be found in an imaginary tool bag you have been carrying and possibly didn't know you had. With you since birth, this imaginary bag has always been ready for you to open it and use the tools inside.

These were the best tools for everything in your life, whether it was an education, a career, or a family. You were using these gifts in your life when tasks, situations, and challenges were easy for you. So you knew you had some tools for something, but probably didn't know what they were or what purpose they were to serve. Now you will name them and know them.

Personal gifts are the tools used to share your vision, express your purpose, and live your mission.

Personal gifts determine the quality of actions or experiences, not the actions themselves. Actions arising from your gifts are marked by ease, lightness, energy, and impact. When you are using your gifts, you are absorbed in what you are doing, totally present and enjoying it. The quality of your actions and responses from your gifts is high and steeped in passion. People experiencing your gifts note what you easily do or know. Often they are in awe or express admiration for the ease of your efforts.

Actions in opposition to your gifts are difficult, frustrating, boring, and draining. When you are not using your gifts, you may want to get away from a situation or task. This will be characterized by your focus on measuring how long something takes, how much you get paid, or when it will be over.

Especially in work situations, most people use their gifts between 40–70% of the time, depending on what they are doing. When people are spending more than 50% of their time on tasks, projects, or situations that don't allow them to use their gifts, they feel stressed and trapped, and will eventually get burned out.

Most days, the ideal situation is to have 80–90% of your time and energy utilizing your gifts in some way. When this happens, people say they can't believe they get paid to do what they do because they love it so much. This maximum use of gifts is intended for each of us. Gifts matter, and knowing more about yours can change everything in your life, especially what you do as work to generate income.

Gifts will also affect your relationships, recreational interests, hobbies, and other activities. We will expand these ideas when we talk about using your plan to live your life at the end of *The Guide*.

Gifts are easier to identify, and especially differentiate, when you recognize what they are not. Personal gifts are not skills. If you are being trained or have been trained in skills to work in the world, society has told you that those skills are the ticket to your success. You may have learned skills to draw a house plan, teach math, or write a book. You may have experience using skills to repair an engine, make a cake, or organize files. We can all learn such skills, but the quality of those skills will vary greatly.

Most people have learned a whole range of skills that may or may not be useful in living their life plan. The real secret to success with skills is a match between skills and personal gifts. Every personal gift has a range of skills that are made easy because of the gift, or difficult without it. This is true in the learning, using, and mastering of skills.

When a skill is easy and you master it and use it effectively, it is because a gift is sitting underneath the skill, often without your knowledge. When you know your gifts, you can identify the skills that will be easily learned and mastered from them, as well as those that will be difficult to learn, and especially master.

When a skill is difficult to learn and master, that skill isn't fully supported by your gifts. This doesn't mean you won't be able to use a skill or improve it; it means that it will be difficult, draining, and often frustrating because it won't come easily. The skills coming from gifts are almost always easy, energizing, and pleasurable. There is a definite difference. Proficient skills come out of gifts, but they are not gifts.

The most magical quality of gifts is that we use them without training, knowledge, or experience, beginning when we are children. Gifts are not dependent on knowledge, but they expand with knowledge and have no limits. Skills can improve with knowledge and experience, especially those derived from gifts, but they will be limited.

You are born with your gifts and they never leave you, but they are easier to use when you have knowledge that makes them more usable. An example might be a gift of being able to see the relationships of color and textures. This gift has probably been used in many situations, from choosing clothes to decorating a living space. This gift and the skills it supports could be expanded and enhanced by training in clothing design or interior design. The gift remains and is useful with or without the expanded knowledge and experience, but is greatly enhanced in effectiveness with knowledge and experience.

After you identify your gifts, we will come back to these concepts of knowledge and skills to show how gifts can affect the world in awesome ways. It will help you to have fun using your gifts with more joy and love. Additionally, the more you are using your gifts, the more opportunities you will attract in which to use them.

You have been given gifts as the tools to effectively live your life plan, make it easy to express your purpose, and especially to do your mission to benefit others in the world. If you are over 25 years old, you already have some pretty good ideas about what your gifts are because they have been showing up enough for you to know something is there. If you think about what has come easily and been very successful in your life, you may be able see the involvement of your gifts, even without knowing exactly what they are or their names.

Everyone has 3–5 gifts, with the exact number varying from person to person. Again, these are not skills, and the names of the gifts will not sound like skills. Gifts are a combination of two things: what you can do or for whom you do it, and how you can or will do it. Simply put, the name of a gift is a combination of a noun and a verb. Most often this combination can be expressed in two words, but sometimes it is three words.

Once identified, each gift, with its passionate energy, extends itself even more into every area of your life and every situation in which you are involved. Gifts are not only for your professional work or career, where they are critical to success, but they also impact and enhance relationships, special interests, and activities.

It is interesting that our personal gifts are often easier for other people to recognize than they are for us. This happens because others see us differently than we see ourselves. Other people connect who we are with what we do, and vice versa. They also look for the positives in their interactions with us. Most importantly, they look for how we can help, support, or guide them.

Gifts are given to us to give to others, so others experience them that way. A mother or someone who cares for a toddler sees his or her gifts (without knowing the gift names) because they are obvious at that stage in life. Before starting school, children spend every day living from their gifts. Society hasn't yet restricted the use of their gifts by focusing them on skills instead.

Unfortunately, our educational systems bury personal gifts under a cookie-cutter approach to directing people in learning and living. We teach general and specific skill-sets from the assumption that skills are the key to success. Remember, skills can be learned, but they are mastered using gifts. So the cookie-cutter assumption may leave many children frustrated and devastated when skills are difficult for them to learn. This often results in diminishing self-confidence and withdrawal from society.

We can't assume that we can learn the same skills equally or even that we need to learn them. When you know your gifts, you will no longer waste your time and energy on skills and activities that don't match those gifts. Know your gifts and identify the skills they support, and you will know what to do and how to do it to be successful and confident in life. Plus, when you use your gifts to succeed, we all benefit from your gifts and your success.

While the uniqueness of personal gifts can get buried, they are never lost. They will continue to pop up in the classes we are attracted to, the books we enjoy, the activities and groups we want to be part of, and the causes we want to join.

Without identification, gifts can be easily pushed aside in favor of the "should," "must," or "have-to" directions from people and society. Most importantly, we won't know how to use our gifts effectively to make choices about what we do and with whom we do it.

We judge ourselves and our actions or behaviors through a mental filter, comparing who we think we are with who we think we should be. That filter distorts the person we really are and what we can give to the world. This is why most people don't know their life plan, including their vision, purpose, mission, and gifts.

We have been living as who the world told us we were, instead of who we really are. We have censored our gifts or ignored them, even when we had clues about them, dismissing those clues as wishful and unrealistic. Yet, we were feeling there was something else for us.

Now in these exercises you can get a clear view of your gifts as well as some powerful insights into yourself that you have had glimpses of and others have seen in you. For many people, this is often the first time they have really looked. Are you ready to look? You are going to be delighted at what you discover was in your tool kit your entire life!

To begin to identify the names of your 3–5 gifts, you are going to cast a wide net for clues. The language for naming gifts is unusual, but the more exact it is the better. That means starting with lots of words or phrases and choosing the best ones to name your gifts.

For this process, you are going to compile five lists. It is important in asking for and compiling the lists that you follow the instructions exactly as they are written here. If you don't, you will get lists that will make it much harder to find the words and phrases you will need. You may also end up with opinions and censored language, which will not help you to explore the truths about you.

On these five lists will be words and phrases from yourself and people who know you well. You want people to be honest and to include what answers the question or statement, both positive and negative. Request the lists, and once you have them all, return to *The Guide* for instructions on what to do with them. Do not go on in *The Guide* until you have the lists in hand.

Below are the lists and the exact instructions you are to follow in requesting and obtaining them. For all the lists, it is vital that you ask for words and phrases, not sentences.

✪ **List #1**—Your mother, father, or a sibling. Preferably, get this list from your mother if she is willing to provide it for you. Mothers have traditionally had the greatest opportunities to observe children before they began school, so your mother probably knows the details of your childhood best. If not your mother, find a person who spent a lot of time with you *before* you began formal schooling.

Do not tell this person what the list will be used for, as this will bias the answers. You can say you are working on some self-discovery and want to know more about yourself as a young child. Ask this exact question: "What was I like before I started school?" Remember, you need words and phrases, not sentences.

✪ **List #2—A close friend, sibling, partner, or spouse.** Choose someone who has spent a lot of time with you over a long period. This should also be someone who has experienced many situations and challenges with you and has had numerous opportunities to observe you interacting with other people. Again, don't say what the list is for except some self-discovery work. Ask for a list in response to this statement: "Describe me as you know me." As before, ask for words and phrases.

✪ **List #3—A colleague or supervisor.** This should be someone you work with or for, or have worked for over a period of six months or more. It should be a person who has been able to observe you, your work, and your interactions with other people. Once again, don't say what this is for, and ask for a list in response to this statement: "Describe me as you see me as a worker or employee, especially with regard to what and how I do my work." If this is a past colleague or supervisor, change the sentence to: "Describe me as you remember me as a worker or employee, especially with regard to what and how I did my work." Remind them to provide only words and phrases.

✪ List #4—Your Experiences. Spend some time reviewing your experiences in life, including your relationships and work. Describe yourself by completing this statement: "My life experiences are best described as . . . ." Words and phrases for you too, please.

✪ List #5—Your Current Description. For a couple of days, observe your thoughts, feelings, choices, what you like and don't like, and what you enjoy and don't enjoy. Also, be aware of your thoughts about your dreams for the future and what you daydream about doing now. Make a list of words and phrases that fill in the blanks for this statement: "I see myself as . . . , and doing . . . ."

Stop here until you have your lists together, then return to *The Guide* to use them to identify your personal gifts.

These five lists will contain a lot of words and phrases. When you have collected the lists, print or write them out and put them side-by-side on a table. Now look over the lists and do the following:

- Circle the words or phrases that appear more than three times in the lists.
- Group the words or phrases that seem to say the same things together with arrows connecting them to each other.
- Write the words and phrases that appeared more than three times on another sheet of paper.
- Group the words and phrases that were connected or seemed to have the same meaning on a different sheet of paper. Look at each group and circle the word or phrase within the group that best represents the grouping.
- Read aloud the words and phrases you have on the two sheets of paper. As you carefully read them, take a moment to get an internal feel for them. Underline the ones that jump out at you or resonate (feel familiar) with you. Are you starting to get some ideas about your gifts? You are looking for words or phrases that feel like something you easily do. They feel like you and who you are.

You have your lists narrowed down and now have to play, explore, and wonder how the words are connected to you. We will do this with the *Thesaurus* used earlier in *The Guide*. Using your *Thesaurus*, do the following:

- ✲ Looking at the two narrowed lists, which word or phrase is most prominent and resonates with you the most (remember this is an internal feeling, probably somewhere in your heart or gut)? Which is the second word or phrase, and finally the third word or phrase? Write those words and phrases below.

○ Look up each prominent word or phrase in the *Thesaurus*. Note new words that resonate more with you than the word you started with. You may want to take the new words and look them up as well. You are looking for the most powerful words and phrases that resonate with you. As you find them, write them below.

You now have a new list of words that includes some of the same ones from your original lists and some new ones. Look them over and circle the word that you feel is most descriptive of you. Don't worry about the other words. We will come back to them later. First, we want to identify one gift and let you get the feel of the process. Then you can go back and identify the other gifts. For now, focus only on one, probably the most used word or easiest to identify. Write it below.

Above is one word, the one that resonates with you the most. Look at it and say it out loud to yourself. Is your word a noun or a verb? Read both examples below and find the second word to complete your gift. You are looking for a verb to match your noun, or a noun to match your verb.

If your word is a description of something you like or enjoy (noun), look at how you do it. You are looking for an action, the verb part of the gift. For example, if the word is "information or knowledge," what do you do with knowledge or information to serve others?

Maybe you are or have been a teacher, a manager, or a writer. Even though these three are skills, they come out of what you do or could do with knowledge and can lead to more specific things that you did as a teacher, manager, or writer; that is the gift action. Maybe you summarized, organized, or expressed knowledge clearly or in terms others could understand.

There are many possible words; be open to all of them. Play with the words and how they was utilized to easily share your gift with others. Examples may be, "knowledge developer," or "knowledge processor."

If your word was an action or something you did (a verb), look for who or what you did it for, or with. For example, if the word was "organizer," what have you organized that was highly successful, or what did you enjoy organizing? Possibly what you organized was files or papers. Maybe you organized events or groups of people. Examples for this one may be, "space organizer" or "people organizer."

These examples should have started you thinking about your word. You began with a noun (what) and looked for a verb (action), or you began with a verb and looked for a noun. Remember you are looking for what you have done in the past or are doing now that is easy, enjoyable, and serves other people in a very positive way.

Start writing and playing with different word combinations. Resist censoring any of them or looking for the "right" answers. At this moment anything works as a possibility. So go for it. Write your word below and begin to complete the name of the gift by listing all the nouns (what) or verbs (actions) that could go with your word.

Once you start this process of discovering your personal gifts, it is like asking a very profound question; a question that will be answered if you stay open, follow the exercises, and remain light and playful with the process. During this time, listen for words, phrases, stories, songs, advertisements, and comments; anything that seems to ring with you, especially as it relates to the gift you are currently identifying. Whatever it is, make a mental or written note and keep listening. Often some of the best and most accurate gift names show up in very unusual ways, sometimes even "out of the clear blue."

Right now you have some possible gift names that are probably two or three words. Remember there will be a noun and a verb, or "something" that you "do." It is time to leave them alone to let them attract more possibilities and more guidance. This means closing *The Guide* and putting it aside for a day or two.

Stop here until you have some exciting and resonating possibilities, then return to *The Guide* to develop them further.

You have had some time to play with your first gift name and to listen to other possibilities that could identify it for you. In the space below, narrow down your gift description to 2–3 combinations you like. Remember you are looking for a noun and a verb for your gift.

Take what you have, continue the process, and play some more. Sometimes it helps to reverse the words. That means changing the verb to a noun and a noun to a verb. For example, "information organizer," could change to "organizational informer." Go ahead and play with your gift and see if reversing the words gets closer to the gift. If not, stay with the gift you have and go on.

Which of the combinations do you like best? Write it below.

Now that you have narrowed your possibilities down, you are ready to give a name to your first gift and begin to identify the other 2–4 gifts. It is very helpful at this point to go back to your life vision, life purpose, and life mission for review. Because your personal gifts are powerful tools that make it easy for you to follow your life plan, the first three components you have worked on could give you valuable clues to your personal gifts. So rewrite your vision, purpose, and mission below.

My life vision is . . .

My life purpose is . . .

My life mission is . . .

Remember, all components of your life plan flow to and from each other. Your gifts are tools for your vision, purpose, and mission, and thus are very much related. Are there words or phrases in your life plan so far that will help you get clearer about this first personal gift? You can play with the gift again here.

Do you now have a gift name that resonates with you and feels like you have been using it your whole life? Below are examples of three gifts for each of the three people whose life plans have been presented during the previous life plan components. Note how their gifts are the tools for their vision, purpose, and mission.

Their stories have been omitted here because the life plan information is complete enough without them. If you want to review their stories, return to the section on life mission. Otherwise, take a look below at each person's gifts. These gifts are the tools for "doing" their missions, expressing their purposes, and sharing their visions.

Jane M.

Jane's vision is: Everyone is born with a magnificent potential and has full access to a field of possibilities to experience and share their potential.

Jane's purpose is: To guide and inspire people to know and live their potential and possibilities.

Jane's mission is:

1. To provide sensible and usable information and strategies for people to see and easily experience their potential.
2. To design and create programs and materials to help people experience the possibilities that can inspire them.
3. To supply the guidance and support to people who are willing to explore and discover their potential.

Jane's gifts are:

1. Information Synthesizer
2. Insight Generator
3. Barrier Reducer

Bob R.

Bob's vision is: Each day is a new opportunity to create loving connections to what is most important in life.

Bob's purpose is: To make it easier for people to have loving connections to what and who are most important to them.

Bob's mission is:

1. To support and participate in groups that easily connect people to what they love.
2. To encourage people to connect to each other with love and kindness.
3. To design and present materials and programs for parents to honor what is most important through their connections.

Bob's gifts are:

1. Creative Connector
2. Safety Provider
3. Process Smoother

Kate C.

Kate's vision is: People can be happy and successful only when they pursue and live their dreams.

Kate's purpose is: To bring together people, materials, and support so people can experience and live their dreams.

Kate's mission is:

1. To bring the strengths and wisdom of people together.
2. To provide experiences for instant success, on which confidence can be built.
3. To share knowledge and strategies for people to know their dreams and live them.

Kate's gifts are:

1. Bridge Builder
2. Experience Organizer
3. Dream Explorer

Did you notice how different the names of the gifts are from how society generally talks about gifts? In society, what are commonly called gifts are really skills or techniques arising from gifts. The descriptions are unique, but once identified they work very well. They provide clarity with specific guidance unseen in other processes. This is especially important for separating skills from gifts, which will be necessary when changing careers or finding work that is truly you.

Can you recognize the possible skills that might come out of the gifts above? For example, one of my gifts is an *Information Synthesizer*. The development and writing of this book came out of that gift. You are reading information gathered from many sources and years of experience. That information has been synthesized into the process you are following. The skills being used are writing, organizing, designing, and developing. All these skills come from my gift of taking information and synthesizing it for people to use.

If you look at my vision, purpose, and mission above (Jane M.), you can see how this gift and the skills the gift supports help me to share my vision with you, express my purpose, and do my mission by writing this book. Can you see how the components fit together and flow? The components of your life plan will fit together and flow, too.

After looking at the examples above, review the gift you had identified for yourself from the previous exercises. Take a few minutes and list the possible skills that gift would make easy. If you can do this, the gift is clear. If not, it may need more attention.

If you are satisfied, move on to identify a couple other gifts for yourself. Discover the second gift using the process we used before by taking words and phrases from your lists and writing the possible "what" and "action" for each one. Do one at a time and stay with the process until you have identified 2–3 of your gifts. Write them below and continue on.

This process of identifying and clarifying gifts is a fun and rewarding personal treasure hunt. You find a clue, it leads to another clue, and just when you have a pretty good idea where the treasure is, you discover some more clues or the treasure isn't where you thought it would be. Play with this process for your gifts, listen and write, and the gifts will emerge. You will know when you have discovered a gift because it will have the following characteristics:

- You have always done it, easily and automatically.
- You feel fully present when you are using the gift.
- Gaining knowledge and experience using this gift makes the gift even easier to use and more automatic.
- You always get energy from your gift when you are using it, especially in the service of other people.
- You get positive feedback from people about what you are doing or have done for them using

the gift. People are attracted to you and what you are doing when using your gifts during a situation, project, or a task.

- You are not attached to whether others like or approve of the gift or accept it. You share your gifts because they are your gifts, not because of your ego's attachment to what other people think or will do as a result.

- When you are utilizing your gift, you feel inspired, passionate, and happy. You feel connected to what you are using the gift to do and you are inspired to do more.

As you continue working the process in *The Guide* and reviewing your gifts with the other life plan components, your gifts will become more recognizable in your preferences, experiences, and interactions. The gifts will reveal themselves to you, and sometimes it will feel like they are shouting.

Reflect on what you have enjoyed in your life, where your passion has drawn you, and what you have loved doing. It was all your gifts revealing themselves to you. Have fun with your gifts, as they may be the most pleasing discovery of your life.

Best of all, when you know your gifts, you will have real clarity about what you do best and will no longer pursue activities, skills, or tasks that don't match you.

This includes the best work for you, the greatest contributions you can make to the world, and where you can inspire, lead, and help others. It will all be about being who you are using your gifts. Lucille Clifton (poet) summed it up perfectly when she said, "In the bigger scheme of things the Universe is not asking us to *do* something, the Universe is asking us to *be* something. And that's a whole different thing."

Write out the names of your gifts below, as you know them now. If you have one, two, or three, that is fine (there is space for them). If you don't, that is fine, too. Other gifts will present themselves later, sometimes not until you know the entire plan and have begun following it in your life. Don't get concerned if you only have a couple; the rest will come when it is time.

Later, when we talk about how to use your life plan, we will discuss how to use your gifts to identify or create work, a career, or a profession that will bring you great joy. So write the gifts below and let's move on to the next component.

Gift #1

Gift #2

Gift #3

Your Personal Standards

You now have a life vision, purpose, mission, and a few personal gifts identified. To have your life plan act as a compass and point the way for your daily choices, you will need one more important tool. This tool will aid the alignment of your path of daily living with your life plan.

Some people call this tool "values," but the concept of values has been so misused in society that using the typical values of society as a guide can be confusing and even take you away from your life plan. That isn't to say that some of the values in society are not useful and important. It is to say that as currently discussed, taught, and used in our society, values can be difficult to sort out. For your life plan, we are going to call this important tool "standards," and sometimes "guides."

Standards are your personal directions for behavior, guides for interactions, and filters for choices and decisions.

Our personal standards have specific characteristics that separate them from beliefs, principles, goals, and other words used to clarify directions in our lives. This powerful component in your life plan shows the way for you to experience joy and live a peaceful and loving life. Think of standards as *where you will stand* in every situation or experience.

You are born with your standards and they support your life plan. This makes your standards personal and unique to you when combined with the other life plan components. Standards are not learned, nor do they change over a lifetime. You will change however, as you discover your standards and choose actions from their guidance.

Other people may have standards with the same names or may even have some of the same standards statements. It will be the composition of your standards and their relationship to the other components in your life plan that will make them unique. They will smooth your life path by uniquely guiding you to the way that is the best and right one for following your life plan.

The best characteristics of standards can be found in our behavior, actions, and choices. When we are behaving in alignment with our standards, we don't judge, harm, manipulate, or attempt to control other people. Additionally, we hold no expectation for other people to abide by our standards. Our personal standards are the guides for our own choices and for respecting other people's choices in our interactions with them.

You will never harm another person by living and choosing from your standards. Your standards will provide the clearest guide for how you should conduct yourself in situations, relationships, and work. That means your standards will not depend on the approval or permission of others. Your standards are your best guides because they are the best way for you to fully share your vision, express your life purpose, fulfill your mission, and use your gifts. Before you look at your standards, there are some critical concepts to understand about them and how you will depend on them to live on the path of your life plan.

As previously mentioned, standards are not societal values. Most values in society are beliefs passed from one generation to the next, not because they are true, but because they are known and believed. Beliefs can also originate in the rules and dogmas of a specific group such as a political or professional group, religion, or a cultural tradition. Such beliefs can be held as truths to apply to everyone and thus be used to judge, separate, or even harm others who don't subscribe to those beliefs.

Especially today, such values have become the criteria for goodness, approval, and inclusion with the effects of marginalizing, hurting, and punishing people who don't meet the criteria. The effects of your standards will be kindness, love, and compassion. You will have no need to label behavior as evil or wrong, or to make judgments about yourself or others. Your standards will be your responsibility and will be used to do the best and right thing at all times, for you and for others.

Your standards will also guide your responses to the demands, challenges, and expectations of others. Responses are used by your mind to respond to everyday living. They include your thoughts, feelings, words, actions, and behavior patterns. These responses are repeated so much that they become habits, automatically happening without your conscious awareness.

Anyone who has tried to change their habits can testify to how ingrained and automatic they can become. Changing responses and then habits is a process of awareness and consciously choosing different responses. Standards are powerful criteria for consciously choosing to think, feel, speak, act, and behave differently.

Once you know your standards, they will become your personal criteria, especially when you are aware of old responses popping up to respond to experiences, decisions, and interactions. Over time and with repetition, the new responses will become the habits and automatic responses if they are consciously chosen and grounded in your life plan. A useful technique for doing that is to predetermine and design responses that keep your life aligned with your plan.

You can begin to use your standards to make changes in your responses by differentiating between unacceptable, acceptable, and preferred responses for yourself. The objective is to make preferred responses in all aspects of your life. Responses include the thoughts and feelings that reflect your vision, purpose, and mission, as well as the words, actions, and behaviors that clearly demonstrate who you are being from your life plan.

Sometimes however, you may not be able to make preferred responses because situations and interactions may allow only acceptable ones, especially in interactions with other people. Unacceptable responses will be rare and will be a sign for you that you have veered away from your standards, especially when such responses are the result of compromising your standards to accommodate the demands or expectations of other people or situations.

For example, you may prefer to be kind to someone, but they are being defensive and even aggressive towards you. An acceptable response may be to walk away from the situation. An unacceptable response would be to argue with them. You can continue the preferred response of being kind to them, but may then have to choose the acceptable response of walking away.

Still, you will not argue or say things that are judging or attacking.

The effects of your responses will be very different. This technique is useful for almost every choice and response you will need to make on the path of life. Responding from your standards will always be the best choice, even when others may not understand your choices and your responses. Remember, personal standards do not require the approval or acceptance of other people. They are in essence non-negotiable for you as the guides for your responses.

When you are in conflict with your standards you will know right away. Your thoughts, feelings, words, actions, and behavior patterns will be negative. You will feel like you are struggling, conflicted, and confused. It can be said that most negativity and difficulty in our lives is the result of responding contrary to our personal standards.

When you don't feel good about something you are doing or not doing, your responses are contrary to your standards. This does not make standards a test, only a guide. You will first be aware of contrary responses when you are reflecting on what previously happened. As you follow your standards more closely, you will know immediately or right after an experience when you are responding contrary to your standards.

Eventually your standards will direct your responses automatically because they are who you are. When not sure, ask yourself a simple question, "What is the best and right thing to do?" Your standards will provide the answer as the best choice and the best response.

What you will say "yes" to will be congruent with your standards. You will say "no" to what is contrary to your standards. This sounds simple because it is. Your standards will empower you to say, "No, I will not do that," or "No, thank you." Remember, standards are your personal guides to joy and love. They make every choice in life clearer and easier, including responses. They are your key to accessing and maintaining your full power and your happiness.

Another important aspect of standards is that they help you to see what matters most in your life. They help you to separate the trivial from the important. This means more opportunities, situations, and requests can be immediately seen as fitting who you are and what is best for you, or not fitting and not being good for you in the long run. There will be no wrong or right, just "bests." You are now ready to know your bests by identifying your standards.

Standards are statements of what is most important to you. They have names, but it is the statement that makes them effective. Everyone has 8–12 standards or guides. Each statement also has an essence that is the core of the standard and usually consists of one or two words.

No matter how many times you revisit and revise your standards statements, the core essence will remain pretty much intact. This will make more sense as you follow the exercises and especially when you "test-drive" your standards in life situations. For now, let's start identifying the names of your standards by answering this very important question. List words only, no sentences please.

> *What is most important to you that you greatly value, and speaks to who you are or want to be in all areas of your life?*

Review the words you just wrote and cross off specific people, things, or objects. From the remaining words, which words are descriptive or have powerful meanings to you? Circle those. Do they lead you to other possible words for what is most important to you? Add them in the space above. Read the list aloud and feel each word for its resonance with you. In the space below, write a new list of the words that describe what is most important to you.

These words tell you what is most important because they are the most powerful for you. These words describe the guides you have been following, often without your acknowledgement. Keep the words in mind as you answer the two following questions:

What would you choose to do if you knew your life would end in the next six months?

What would you give your time and energy to if you knew you had the resources do so without limitation?

From these questions, you are getting more clues about what is most important to you and who you are being when you are at your best. Below is a list of common names for standards. Circle 20–25 that you like from your lists or the questions above, or new ones that resonate for you. You can also add words to the list to get your 20–25 words.

Abundance	Acceptance	Achievement
Action	Adventure	Appreciation
Balance	Beauty	Caring
Challenge	Change	Choices
Collaboration	Commitment	Community
Compassion	Connection	Consistency
Cooperation	Courage	Creativity
Dependability	Determination	Discovery
Diversity	Efficiency	Effort
Empathy	Empowerment	Endurance
Equality	Excellence	Experience
Exploration	Fairness	Faith
Family	Friendship	Flow
Focus	Fun	Gratitude
Harmony	Health	Honesty

Hope	Humor	Independence
Information	Initiative	Inspiration
Integrity	Intimacy	Justice
Knowledge	Learning	Liberty
Love	Loyalty	Mastery
Order	Opportunity	Optimism
Peace	Perseverance	Persistence
Pleasure	Potential	Power
Precision	Refinement	Relationships
Resilience	Respect	Responsibility
Risk	Safety	Security
Self-sufficiency	Serenity	Service
Sharing	Spirituality	Strength
Success	Support	Tolerance
Tradition	Truth	Trust
Unity	Wealth	Wisdom
Work		

Now reduce your list by circling the fifteen words about which you feel strongest. You may have to give this some thought and may want to leave the exercise now and come back later to look at the list again. You can also get out the *Thesaurus* you used for the gifts section to look up some of the words.

When you are satisfied with your top fifteen words, list them on the left side of the page below, leaving space on the right side to write next to each one. These will be the names of your standards for now. Don't worry about the words you didn't include, as you will come back and clarify the words and the statements of your standards more than a few times, so they may return later. For now, let's see what you have and get started writing each standard and its statement.

With your words or names of your standards listed on the left side of the page, take each word and write a definition or phrase that expresses how you feel about the word. What does it mean? For example, if one of your words was health, the definition or statement might read: *Health is the balance between nutrition, fitness, and rest.*

The statements don't have to be exact and are only a beginning, so write whatever comes to mind. You can use a dictionary if it will help you get started. For each standard name, you want to have a word and a statement or definition like the example above. They will read, "health is," or "truth is," etc.

Then keep rephrasing, adding to, or deleting from the statement to make it a more powerful representation of what is most important to you. Write each of your standard's name and definition or statement below.

Give yourself time to experiment with these statements by rewriting them. You will find them overlapping and even conflicting with each other. That is part of the clarification process. You may find that you have two standards that say the same thing. If so, collapse them into one and choose the standard name that works best. You can also change the names or statements if you want. These statements are more powerful than just a definition or sentence. State what is important to you as clearly as you can for now.

When you have your list and first pass at the statements ready, you can reduce it again to make your standards even more concise. Study your standards and reduce your list to ten. Do this by looking for similarity within some, or for those that don't seem as important now. List the ten standards you have chosen as your top ones below. Include each standard's name and the standard's statement.

Read your ten standards out loud and listen for a key word for each one. There is a word that captures the essence of each standard. It probably has a resonance or emotional charge to it. Think back to the previous example: *Health is the balance between nutrition, fitness, and rest.* Can you see the key word? For this standard named *Health*, the key word or essence is *balance*.

Circle the key word in each of your standard's statements above. If you can't decide on one essence word, two will be okay for now. Write the name of each standard with the essence or key word next to it below. We are setting the statements temporarily aside. You will only have a standard name and an essence word for each one.

When discovering your standards, the process is one of contraction and expansion. You started with a word and added a statement (expansion). Then we took the statements and chose an essence word (contraction). Let's expand again.

This time you will write the name of the standard and rewrite the statement for it, emphasizing the essence or key word. You may end up with the same statement you had before, or a new one. Keep the statement focused and supportive of the essence word.

Additionally, if you had a definition before, turn it into a statement. It is helpful to begin the statement with the name of the standard and the word "is" (see previous example). Write the new standards below, with the name of the standard followed by the statement containing and focusing on the essence word.

Your standards now need more clarity and a "test-drive." Trying them out in your current life will help you clarify them as well as test them for their truth and importance to you. First, reflect on two recent experiences; one experience which was positive and enjoyable, and one which was negative and not enjoyable.

Start with the enjoyable experience and replay in your mind what you were doing, where you were, and what happened. Which of your ten standards above guided you in the situation? This guidance can be recognized by the choices you made, what you said, or how you interacted with other people. If you enjoyed the situation, you were aligned with some of your personal standards. It could have been one, two, or even more.

With which of your standards were you most aligned? Here is an example of how to take a standard for a "test-drive" and get more clarity.

Standard

Health is the balance between nutrition, fitness, and rest.

Positive Situation

I got together with some friends to take an all-day hike in a national park. The hike was challenging and the interactions enjoyable. Sharing good food added to the positive experience, and resting above the canyon was inspiring. Clarity came to me with the realization that activities that combine and balance nutrition, challenging physical activity, and rest that inspires, are the most enjoyable for me. The *Health* standard guided all my choices for the day and resulted in a joyful experience.

Recall the positive experience you were thinking about when asked earlier. Write the standard or standards and how you were aligned with it or them below:

Standard(s)

Positive Situation

Let's look at negative experiences and how they are the result of choices that are contrary to our standards. Here is the same standard of *Health* used as an example before, but in a different experience—this time not following the standard.

Standard

Health is the balance between nutrition, fitness, and rest.

Negative Situation

I attended a party that offered a variety of foods and social interactions. It was not enjoyable because I ate too much food that was not nutritional, stayed too long, and had difficulty meeting new people—I felt trapped. Had the standard for health been followed, I would have eaten before going to the party and then chosen foods at the party more carefully. Also, I would have gone home at a reasonable time and taken a more relaxed and curious approach to meeting new people. The clarity from the experience is to know what is most important and set boundaries to align with it, no matter what I perceive the outside or inside social pressures to be.

Write the recent negative experience you were asked to recall below. What standard or standards were in conflict with your behavior and choices? What would you have done differently had you been in alignment with your standards? What is the clarity you have for what happened and living your standards?

Standard(s)

Negative Experience

Our life experiences, and especially our responses and choices, either follow our personal standards or are contrary to them. Like most people, you probably weren't aware of your personal standards; you only knew that the experience went well or it didn't. You may have felt guilty or beat yourself up about what happened. You may have also blamed the situation or another person for what happened to you.

One of the most powerful aspects of knowing and following your life plan is that you will accept and relish taking responsibility for your life and your experiences. When you take responsibility for your experiences you will no longer blame anyone or anything, or have confusion about what happened. You will know that the compass of your life plan will guide your choices and you will have the tools of gifts and standards to make the best choices. While that may seem a little daunting at this moment, in time you will find it to be extremely empowering and freeing.

That was your first test-run with your personal standards. Take a couple of days and reflect on other situations or experiences and look again for alignment and conflict with your standards in your choices and behavior. As you become more familiar with your standards and their application in your life, you will recognize where they need clarifying in their language, or when new standards need to be added and others removed.

Every experience involves your personal standards. If you can't find at least one standard that fits, then a standard is missing from your group or more clarity of your current standards is needed. Below, clarify your standards by rewriting them. You may also add or remove some. You should have somewhere between eight and twelve standards that are solid guides for you in every situation.

As you clarify and hone your standards, you will find yourself thinking about them more. Better still, you will begin to recognize their useful guidance for your life. However, we need to do one more expansion before moving on to the next plan component.

While you probably have one sentence for each of your standards, you may have considered having a couple of sentences. You can add those now. You may need more than one sentence to fully state what is important and capture the essence of your standards.

Think of this as a statement of who you will be, what you will do, and how you will do what you do in your experiences. Taking the previous "health" example from before, if it was expanded it would look like this:

> *Health is the balance between nutrition, fitness, and rest. Healthy daily choices provide the consistency of balance and optimum health.*

The added emphasis on choices explains how balance is maintained. Take another look at your standards statements and expand them below if necessary.

Now that you have written a group of standards for your plan, let's return to the three examples of life plans used previously in *The Guide* to see how a life plan continues to reveal itself with some standards included. For brevity, only three of the standards for each plan are included. The actual plans have more, but these three will be enough to illustrate how the life plan and the components fit together. Notice again the flow from vision to purpose to mission, and how the tools of gifts and standards support and provide guidance for a daily path to follow each life plan.

Jane M.

Jane's vision is: Everyone is born with a magnificent potential and has full access to a field of possibilities to experience and share their potential.

Jane's purpose is: To guide and inspire people to know and live their potential and possibilities.

Jane's mission is:

1. To provide sensible and usable information and strategies for people to see and easily experience their potential.

2. To design and create programs and materials to help people experience the possibilities that can inspire them.

3. To supply the guidance and support to people who are willing to explore and discover their potential.

Jane's gifts are:

1. Information Synthesizer
2. Insight Generator
3. Barrier Reducer

Jane's standards include:

1. *Human potential* is the ultimate expression of living the possibilities available to each

person. Each day, choices should expand and affirm a person's potential.

2. *Possibilities* are the endless ways, resources, and opportunities for creating anything and everything. Seeing possibilities is the power to create.

3. *Inspiration* is the connection between possibilities and potential. Environments, relationships, and experiences should invite and nourish inspiration.

Bob R.

Bob's vision is: Each day is a new opportunity to create loving connections to what is most important in life.

Bob's purpose is: To make it easier for people to have loving connections to what and who are most important to them.

Bob's mission is:

1. To support and participate in groups that easily connect people to what they love.

2. To encourage people to connect to each other with love and kindness.

3. To design and present materials and programs for parents to honor what is most important through their connections.

Bob's gifts are:

1. Creative Connector
2. Safety Provider
3. Process Smoother

Bob's standards include:

1. *Relationships* are grounded in connections. Honoring those connections honors each person and deepens relationships.
2. *Self-knowledge* is the loving gift brought to all relationships. Everything is possible and resolvable through this self-knowledge.
3. *Safe environments* are open, honest, supportive, and caring ones for individuals to take risks and grow personally and collectively.

Kate C.

Kate's vision is: People can be happy and successful only when they pursue and live their dreams.

Kate's purpose is: To bring together people, materials, and support so people can experience and live their dreams.

Kate's mission is:

1. To bring the strengths and wisdom of people together.
2. To provide experiences for instant success, on which confidence can be built.
3. To share knowledge and strategies for people to know their dreams and live them.

Kate's gifts are:

1. Bridge Builder
2. Experience Organizer
3. Dream Explorer

Kate's standards include:

1. *Lifelong learning* increases the possibilities for living dreams and having fulfilling experiences. Every experience can be a learning experience.
2. *Confidence* is the knowledge of what has been achieved and is possible. With confidence, all risks are only expanded opportunities.

3. *Independence* is the freedom to determine success by taking responsibility for choices and behavior.

After reviewing the examples above, did you take another look at the standards you had written? If you did, you probably made changes and found some affirmation for the standards you had written for yourself.

This is a good time to test-drive them in current and upcoming situations. Think about an upcoming experience and consider how you will apply your personal standards to the choices, decisions, or actions you are going to be taking or making.

Aligned with your personal standards, what would you do, say, not do, not say, choose, or decide in your biggest life decisions? Look closely at your written standards as you consider the possibilities.

People who don't rely on their standards often rely on the common approach of making a list of pros and cons for decision-making. This method assumes difficult choices, actions, and options can be mathematically determined by either more pros or more cons. While you may have had some success with this method, following your personal standards is much more effective for deciding anything and everything.

When you align with your personal standards and the other components of your life plan, you will always know what to do and it will be the best and right thing to do now and in the future. And yes, other people may not like your choices, but in the long run using your standards will always guide you to the best results.

As you clarify and know your standards, you will have daily opportunities to use them for guidance. As you use them, your experiences will let you know when your standards need clarification or their application needs to be clearer.

Also, as your personal standards become your guides for your life and experiences, they will overlap more or take primary or secondary roles. That means one standard may be the main one you are using, but a few others are taking complementary roles in the decision or choice.

Over time, the more you trust and rely on your personal standards, the more automatic they will become and the less it will matter which one you use. Your personal standards or guides will guide your path and be the foundation for your integrity.

You will know you are choosing from a standard because these choices will be positive, focused, and powerful, and they will express your life vision and purpose well. Standards are the keys to living a life you can be proud of—one that fully maximizes your life plan to make a loving and joyful contribution to the world.

As we leave this section on personal standards, let's see how your life plan looks now. Below, rewrite the components of your life plan as you know them.

My life vision is . . .

My life purpose is . . .

My life mission is . . .

My personal gifts are . . .

My personal standards are . . .

There is one more component to your life plan that is contrary to all the others. Yes, contrary to them. It is the back-up component of the plan. Before we explore it, please review the five components you have completed and consider their relationship to each other.

You may recall in the beginning of *The Guide*, it was stated that the first three components flow into each other. So the life purpose flows from the vision, and the mission flows from the purpose. The gifts and standards are the tools for using your life plan, or the compass to navigate the path for your life.

Look back at what you have written above. Does it flow? Do the tools direct the path and make sense for sharing your vision, expressing your purpose, and doing your mission? You should also be able to feel how it resonates with what you have done in your life and what you passionately now want to do.

It is suggested that you then write the plan on a 3x5" index card and carry it with you in your purse, bag, or pocket. Write the vision, purpose, mission, and gifts on one side of the card. On the other side of the card, write your personal standards. Several times over the next few days, take out the card, read it, and consider your alignments with or departures from your plan each day. You can also make changes on the card as you go, and transfer them back into *The Guide* later. This is a good time to do some tweaking and rewriting.

There is one important reminder here. Our personal life plan reveals itself as we discover, explore, and live it. It gets clearer as we go and easier to live. You will make a number of changes as you complete *The Guide*, and continue making changes in the months and years to come. It won't be that the plan is changing; you will be changing. The plan will get clearer and more precise. As you change, you will remember what you have always known: there is a plan for your life that will bring you joy and love in the service of others.

When you are confident with what you have, write the plan below. You will want to be pretty sure of the first five components before we challenge them with the last component.

My life vision is . . .

My life purpose is . . .

My life mission is . . .

My personal gifts are . . .

My personal standards are . . .

Stop here and reconsider, rework, and reflect on your plan. Return to *The Guide* in a few days to discover and explore the powerful last component.

Your Personal Ego-Mind

Your life plan is the compass for guiding your choices to a life filled with joy and love. If you follow the direction your compass points, your days will be rich with meaning as you share your joy and love in the service of the world. That is the purpose of your life.

However, as with all great plans, there is a backup or failsafe component built into your life plan. It is a plan within the plan, to guarantee you always have a guide for your life. This secondary plan is called the ego-mind. Not grounded in a vision, purpose, and mission or a guide to love and joy, the ego-mind guides daily living using a powerful tool called egoic needs.

The intention of the ego-mind is survival, while hoping for experiences in happiness and fulfillment. This is quite different than the intention of your life plan, yet your ego-mind's plan can be vital and highly functional when:

- As a child, you don't have the knowledge or experience to know how to live your life plan.
- You don't discover or explore your plan (most people haven't).
- You wander off your intended path and away from your life plan. This is easy to do even when you know your plan and the path it directs you to.

There was such a high probability that this backup component of your life plan would be necessary, that it was infused with a lot of power and an effective illusionary quality. The ego-mind's plan is so powerful that most people live their entire lives believing it is the guide for their lives.

> *The ego-mind is the protector and director of your perception of reality and identity: who you think you are, or "me." The ego-mind persistently pursues and defends the illusion of happiness.*

Beginning at birth, the ego-mind was the first component of your life plan revealed to you, formulating your personal identity or how you would think of yourself (remember you had a blue or pink blanket). Almost immediately, your parents, family, and others started impressing upon you their idea of who you were and who you were supposed to be. They used reward and punishment to make clear what you could and could not do, and your ego-mind was listening and responding to them.

Being only a child with no sense of who you were or who you could be, of course you believed those surrounding and caring for you, internalizing what they and the greater society repeated to you about you. Your identity crystallized, and your ego-mind continued to process the perceived information as evidence confirming your identity.

The ego-mind developed a rapid and efficient system of selectively sorting into meanings and relevance the flood of information gathered by your senses. From the masses of perceptual data, it plucked what was useful and allowed the rest to be stored by the brain.

Before long, interpretations were automatically made to fit the current version of your identity, whether the interpretations were factual or not. The ego-mind fit this identity into a false but convincing reality, which became your personal reality.

As you aged, the efficiency of these interpretations and the responses they triggered to protect and defend your identity and reality formed everything you believed about yourself and what you could, couldn't, should, and shouldn't do. This worked, and would continue to work as long as you didn't question your identity and reality or know your life plan.

The limitation of your ego-mind's perpetuated reality and identity is that it is a powerful barrier to living your intended life plan. Filling in for your intended plan, your ego-mind has inklings about the greater life plan, but doesn't recognize how those inklings fit together or even what they mean.

Have you ever heard something or had a feeling or intuitive insight that resonated with you at some level, but you didn't know what it meant? You knew you were being prompted in some way, even inspired, but couldn't put your finger on what it meant or what to do with it. Those were probably inklings about your life plan. But your ego-mind didn't recognize them as part of what it perceived as reality, so it ignored or dismissed them as fantasies or wishful thinking. You were reminded to get back to "reality."

These inklings were coming from a deeper place than your ego-mind could currently perceive: the source of your life plan. Introduced at the beginning of *The Guide*, this source is often referred to as God, Spirit, Source, or Creator. Some call it the Universal Mind, Oneness, or a Higher Power. Whatever name we attribute to this source, most people seem to have an awareness of something deeper and richer than the ego-mind or "me." If this weren't true, there would be no need or reason for a life plan. But you know there is, or you wouldn't still be reading this book.

It is our ego-mind that keeps us from connecting to the source of our life plan and consequently from who we truly are and were intended to be. The power of your life plan comes from knowing the purpose for your life as well as the joy and love you can experience and share following that plan. Even though the ego-mind is a barrier to your true self and a protector of a false self, this doesn't mean that it is evil, in opposition to your life plan, or anything like that.

Your ego-mind is a secondary or backup plan always ready to guide you when you don't follow or don't know your intended life plan. Even when you know and follow your life plan, your ego-mind will be ready just in case you forget the primary plan or wander off the path. Your ego-mind can immediately slide forward as your guide to preserve and defend the identity and reality it already knows.

The ego-mind perceives, defends, and protects a false identity and reality using what it knows best—the past. This identity and reality is your story, with you as the main character and the people with whom you have relationships as the secondary characters. Central to your story is your education or training, your work and career, and how your security and wealth is determined and maintained. Also in your story is your health, specifically your body image and the meaning of your body to who you think you are. Your story is what you project every day in every choice and interaction. It is you, but only if you don't know your life plan.

Even though your story is based solely on your past, it is the foundation for your present. You are convinced that you are here right now, but your ego-mind is just projecting your story with the old reality, old interpretations, and previous responses into the present. The mind's best technique is to repeat what has already happened. Not very creative, the ego-mind does what is easiest, which is to repeat responses (thoughts, feelings, words, actions, and behavior patterns) already locked into your identity and reality.

Since the ego-mind only knows a false reality or your story, it anticipates the present and future with trepidation and is very threatened by any possible changes that could affect the story, reality, and identity. So comfortable with what it believes, the ego-mind can only fear anything it perceives to threaten the reality it knows. Fear is the currency of the ego-mind and it reacts fearfully whenever it anticipates anything in the future or even a minute from now. Oscar Wilde, the playwright, could have been describing the power of the ego-mind when he boldly stated, "Most people are other people. Their thoughts are someone else's opinions, their lives a mimicry, their passions a quotation."

While your ego-mind was developing and expanding, it was relying on a powerful tool to keep you believing the identity and reality it had formed and was protecting. This tool is called your egoic needs and doesn't include your physical needs such as hunger, shelter, or sleep. Egoic needs are psychological needs operating mostly outside your conscious awareness, driving and prompting your daily choices and responses. Their purpose is always to protect and maintain your identity and current reality.

While it may seem at times that there are subordinate needs underneath them, they all lead back to three core egoic needs perpetuating the story of who you are and what is important to you. Egoic needs are grounded in your belief system, which is formed and reformed throughout your life. Beliefs are an array of learned principles and definitions you have accepted as truths due to their constancy and repetition. Many beliefs are useful and lead to choices that are beneficial, such as beliefs about health and rest, or beliefs about responsibility and treating other people with respect.

However, there is a group of beliefs that are not useful, that minimize your power, and that lead to choices which limit your possibilities and (most importantly) keep you from following your life plan. These beliefs are called limiting beliefs.

Limiting beliefs are negative because they protect a false identity defining what you can't do or who you are not. They support your story by defining your potential and what you can expect in your life. Limiting beliefs originated within your family and were conditioned and reinforced through repeated feedback from other people and your experiences. Limiting beliefs then frame your current experiences to make sure you carefully avoid anything that you can't do or that might be uncomfortable. The ego-mind relies on them for interpreting experiences to supply workable responses or choices, which are further limiting, but comfortable and safe.

What do these limiting beliefs look like? They are frames through which every experience is viewed. For example, a common limiting belief is that success is achieved by being better than others, and if you are not the best you are not successful. Another limiting belief that paralyzes people is that taking a risk is likely to lead to failure and embarrassment, so it is best to play it safe and stick to what you know you can do. Yet another common limiting belief is that happiness is determined by what you have and own; therefore, if you don't have what other people have, you can't be happy.

Each of us has a long list of limiting beliefs that frame our experiences. Which limiting beliefs are framing your experiences? You can discover your limiting beliefs because they enter your mind whenever you consider making a change or taking action to go for something bigger than you currently believe you can do or achieve. They are the chorus of voices reminding you of what you should avoid in your experiences.

Your life plan needs no protection, and when followed will guide choices and experiences by framing them within your vision, purpose, mission, and standards. If you know your limiting beliefs, you can recognize what is in the way of living your plan—especially those egoic needs being used to guide your choices in place of the standards and gifts inherent within your life plan. When it comes to the ego-mind, the more you know about what it is doing and how it is doing it, the less power it has to keep you from your life plan.

Let's look more closely at how your ego-mind uses egoic needs to protect and defend a false identity and reality; keep you in your story; and prevent you from living your life plan. The purpose of your egoic needs is to seek what is perceived to be missing or lacking (usually outside of you), which if possessed, understood, or done could bring wholeness or completeness in some aspect of your life. The illusion of something missing or lacking allows the mind to continue looking, doing, getting, and hoping.

Egoic needs do not lead to wholeness, but rather to a continuing perception that something more is missing and must be pursued. The only path to wholeness lies in living your life plan, with the subsequent joy and love confirming you are already whole.

We can see the effects of egoic needs in our lives without recognizing the needs that are operating. For example, wanting to please others so they will not be disappointed in us comes from the egoic need for approval. We want to please others because we believe that if other people are happy, we can be happy. If they are unhappy, we can't be happy. The ego-mind wasn't really interested in the happiness of others as much as it was interested in what would make us happy.

Becoming aware of your egoic needs and limiting beliefs brings them out of the "shadow" where they are operating. A term used by Carl Jung, the Swiss psychologist, the shadow is the hidden area of the ego-mind where fear is born and limiting beliefs reside. The only way to expose the powerful beliefs and fears hidden in the shadow is to shine light on what the shadow is hiding. Awareness is that light.

The more aware you are of your egoic needs and the behaviors they drive, the less power they have on your responses. And then you can consciously choose to respond differently. The shadow has a lot to teach you about your fears and limiting beliefs. Awareness without judging your shadow's contents can be very liberating and enlightening.

What is in the shadow is not bad, but protective and useful when you are not following your life plan. Just reading this section can begin to bring your egoic needs into your awareness by highlighting the source of much of your behavior. This can be very valuable. At the end of *The Guide* you will learn how to fulfill your egoic needs and decrease their power and the power of the shadow even more. For now, there is some other information that will increase your awareness and help you see how limiting beliefs, egoic needs, and the ego-mind function together in your story.

There are three egoic needs driving the majority of your behavior. By driving behavior, egoic needs maintain a congruency between who you are and what you do. They keep your story alive and very realistic. Remember, this sense of identity is a false self, so the behaviors originating from it are often false, too—they are not the true you.

The true you is the one sharing your life vision, expressing your purpose by how you are showing up in the world, doing your mission, and using your gifts and standards. The egoic mind has a different purpose—the perpetuation and continuing expression of your identity and reality. When you follow the path guided by your life plan, you will have a new identity which will lead you to interact with the world from love instead of fear. This is quite a different place.

To clear the way for your new identity of love, let's identify your egoic needs. Of your three egoic needs, you have one in common with everyone else: the need for approval or acceptance. Sometimes called love, achievement, or validation, it is still the same need. For our discussion, we will call it the need for approval.

This primary egoic need drives the majority of your behavior throughout your life. To illustrate how your needs are operating in your life right now, we are going to focus on your need for approval. We will come back to your other two needs later.

The power of an egoic need is the source of its energy, which is fear. Egoic needs are like a coin; they have two sides, yet appear as one. The need for approval has a flipside (like a coin), which is the fear of rejection. Nothing is more painful to our ego-mind than feeling rejected by other people. This fear is the impetus for us to seek approval, especially from other people.

Seeking approval is a means for avoiding the potential pain and emotional suffering of being rejected and feeling the embarrassment and sadness of being devalued. We will avoid this pain at all costs. So we do what other people want us to do even when we don't want to.

We go places and do things to please others. We sacrifice our health, time, and energy for what others want from us. We melt our personal boundaries because we are afraid of people not liking us if we don't do what they want or give them what they ask for. All these choices hopefully prevent others from rejecting us, and our need to be accepted seems fulfilled. But these choices also conflict with what we want and what we know is best for us.

Egoic needs and the fears on their flipside are direct barriers to living our standards. Even when you know your standards, as you do now, you can still be overwhelmed by the powerful drive of egoic needs and fears. Knowing your needs and being aware of their intrusion into your life reduces their power to operate in the shadow and guide you away from your path to joy. Your awareness opens up possibilities for choosing to respond to other people for reasons other than their approval.

The ego-mind uses your egoic needs to drive you when you are not following your life plan. Egoic needs are also warnings about how your choices are being made, and from what source. As difficult and limiting as the ego-mind sounds, it is quite useful and can be very supportive of your life plan. So we don't want to get rid of the ego-mind; we just want to be aware when it is leading, so we can choose our life plan to lead instead. Additionally, our awareness of the ego-mind, limiting beliefs, and egoic needs can remove the operations of the ego-mind from the shadow.

Let's see what is currently going on in the shadow of your egoic mind. We established earlier that you have three egoic needs and that one of them is your need for approval. The need for approval is energized as a fear of rejection. Let's identify your other two egoic needs and explore the fears on their flipside. You will see how you have been using these needs to drive your behavior and override your standards, all out of the perspective from within the shadow.

Below is a list of possible needs. There are many, but a few of these probably feel familiar to you from your personal experiences. Go ahead and circle 6–8 of the familiar ones to get started. It helps to look at the list and finish these sentences, "I need . . . " or "I need to be . . . ."

Acknowledgement	Activity	Acceptance
Adore	Approval	Authority
Balance	Calm	Certainty
Clarity	Command	Consistency
Control	Create	Devoted
Dominant	Embraced	Exactness
Fitness	Fun	Heard
Importance	Inclusion	Independence

Influence	Liked	Leadership
Love	Loyalty	Obeyed
Observe	Order	Organization
Praised	Peace	Perfect
Possess	Power	Precision
Protection	Responsible	Right
Security	Remembered	Safety
Serenity	Share	Structure
Symmetry	Unity	Validation
Victory	Work	

You have circled a group of 6–8 needs. Please write them below.

Look closely at your list for words that may mean the same thing to you. If you find some, choose the most descriptive one and cross out the others. You may also see that a few words on the list aren't as important to you as you look at them all together. Cross those out, too. Get the list down to 4–5 needs. Your need for approval, or another need meaning the same thing, should be included in that list. Write the final 4–5 words below.

It is time to look at where and how egoic needs have been prominent in your experiences, especially those you considered to be negative experiences with negative outcomes. This will help you to clarify and further identify your three core egoic needs. Answer the following questions:

What were you doing, and where were you, the last time you were anxious, sad, or feeling guilty—even angry?

Think about a relationship that causes you distress and unhappiness. What is it about the relationship and what happens between you and the other person that leaves you feeling out of control or even helpless when interacting with this person?

Reflect on your previous important choices in life such as education, work, and time-consuming activities. What were you feeling when you made a decision or choice to pursue what you did in these areas?

Look at your answers to the three previous questions. What did you need in each of them that would have made you feel better, happier, or more satisfied? Write that below as a word or short phrase.

I needed . . .

I needed . . .

I needed . . .

It is easier to clarify the needs in your experiences by exploring the fears in those experiences. Remember, every need has a fear on its flipside that gives power to the need to drive your behavior. What were you afraid of that drove what you needed above? The following statements will make it easier to identify the need and the fear.

I needed . . .

   because I was afraid that . . .

I needed . . .

   because I was afraid that . . .

I needed . . .

   because I was afraid that . . .

Common needs with their possible fears are shown in the following examples. Check to see if yours are similar, the same, or different.

- ✪ I needed approval because I was afraid of rejection.
- ✪ I needed structure because I was afraid of making mistakes.
- ✪ I needed order because I was afraid of not having control.
- ✪ I needed relationships because I was afraid of being alone.
- ✪ I needed peace because I was afraid of being overwhelmed.
- ✪ I needed control because I was afraid of being weak.
- ✪ I needed to be right because I was afraid of being dumb.

You now have the needs and the fears on their flipsides identified, along with your previous 4–5 needs from the list. Identify three core egoic needs common in both exercises. These are your three egoic needs. Write them below.

I need . . .

I need . . .

I need . . .

Your egoic needs should be clearer now, as well as what they are protecting and preserving in your identity and reality (what you fear). If you had difficulty identifying an egoic need and the fear on its flipside, either the need is not one of yours or it requires you to think more about how you experience it.

It could be helpful to review current situations that cause negative emotions and make you feel bad about what you did or said. Negative emotions (anger, frustration, sadness, guilt, shame) are always clues that a need was operating in your ego's interpretation of the experience. The more you are aware of your needs, the fears behind them, and especially the thoughts, feelings, words, actions, and behavior patterns they produce (responses), the easier it will be to choose something different—your standards.

Let's differentiate between needs and standards since they sometimes have similar or even the same names, which can cause confusion. Remember, the ego-mind is the default or backup component in your life plan. Your life goes on and you live it, but what is guiding it? Will you follow your life plan and the clear path it provides to joy and love? Or, will you follow the lead of the ego-mind, using needs, fears, and limiting beliefs as your mechanisms for guidance?

Think of your standards guiding you and your needs driving you. Since your standards are part of your life plan, their guidance is intended to allow you to have joy and feel love. Needs are the mechanisms of the ego, and their use is intended to protect you from pain and maintain a false reality about who you are. Needs are always about your limiting beliefs and the fear affirming those beliefs.

This is the difference between surviving through the ego and thriving on the intended path for your life. It is the difference between acting *from* your standards and acting *because* of your needs. Your standards provide the freedom to make powerful choices, while your needs drive your choices through your fears to protect an illusion of you.

This leads to an interesting occurrence you are going to experience with your life plan. There will be times when the ego-mind, in order to protect your current identity, will disguise a need and convince you that it is one of your standards. As you live your life plan, you will find yourself having to "tease out" these needs from your standards and vice-versa.

For now, here is a good rule-of-thumb for teasing them out. Any thought, feeling, behavior, or decision that causes conflict, confusion, or drama is coming from an egoic need. Further, needs-driven behavior is typically manipulating, demanding, and pouty or withdrawn. Standards or guides lead to thoughts, behaviors, or decisions that feel positive and get positive, loving, and supportive results. They don't harm others or create dramas and messy situations. Standards will make you feel light, clear, and focused, while needs will make you feel tense, nervous, and expectant.

Another important difference between your needs and standards is the attachment or investment in results or outcomes. When you are choosing from a standard or guide, you will choose because it is the best and right choice for you, regardless of the opinion or judgment of others. When you are choosing from a need, you will be attached to the reactions of others and judge the outcomes or results as good or bad. This is a profound difference and a further guide for knowing whether you are acting from standards or needs.

Additionally, if you doubt your choice, or are weighing your decision because of outcomes and their effects, you are probably considering choices and responses through your needs. This doesn't mean that you should be indifferent or uncaring about the effects of your choices; it just means the criteria for your choices should originate from the best place for you to "stand."

You have to trust that in the long run, the choices or responses from your standards will turn out fine—they always do. Rather than an attachment, this is called having a "vested interest" or being fully responsible for your choices. The more you choose from your standards, the less you will need to defend, have, and avoid.

Even when you know your life plan and are following the path it is directing, you will dance between your standards and your egoic needs. The ego-mind will be quick to fill the void whenever you doubt yourself and your plan. It will rush forward with egoic needs to direct your responses. When you remember who you are and return to trusting the compass of your plan to point the way, the ego-mind will yield to the direction of your life plan. It will also be ready to push forward and drive you almost seamlessly, without your awareness. Emotions, intentions, and awareness will be the indicators of whether you are choosing what is best and right, or what is needed.

Hopefully, that helped to clarify your egoic needs and how they operate within your life plan—sometimes in replacement of it. Review the three egoic needs you identified earlier. It will help to put the fear or flipside next to each one. When you know the fear, you will know when a need is driving your choices. Write them below. If you have changed them after that brief discussion on standards and needs, finalize them here.

I need . . .   (fear of . . .   )

I need . . .   (fear of . . .   )

I need . . .   (fear of . . .   )

Let's put your egoic needs with the rest of your life plan and see how it flows together now. Carry forward what you know is in your life plan and add your egoic needs below.

My life vision is . . .

My life purpose is . . .

My life mission is . . .

My gifts are . . .

My standards are . . .

My egoic needs are . . .

We are going to revisit the life plans of Jane, Bob, and Kate to see how their egoic needs and their ego-minds can interfere with following their life plans. There is a brief section following their egoic needs which explains what happens when they live from their needs instead of their standards. With the ego-mind taking the lead, notice that it potentially affects the path for following their life plans and can even neutralize their life plans. They would still be effective, but they would be negatively affected and their impact limited.

Jane M.

Jane's vision is: Everyone is born with a magnificent potential and has full access to a field of possibilities to experience and share their potential.

Jane's purpose is: To guide and inspire people to know and live their potential and possibilities.

Jane's mission is:

1. To provide sensible and usable information and strategies for people to see and easily experience their potential.

2. To design and create programs and materials to help people experience the possibilities that can inspire them.

3. To supply the guidance and support to people who are willing to explore and discover their potential.

Jane's gifts are:

1. Information Synthesizer
2. Insight Generator
3. Barrier Reducer

Jane's standards include:

1. *Human potential* is the ultimate expression of living the possibilities available to each person. Each day, choices should expand and affirm a person's potential.
2. *Possibilities* are the endless ways, resources, and opportunities for creating anything and everything. Seeing possibilities is the power to create.
3. *Inspiration* is the connection between possibilities and potential. Environments, relationships, and experiences should invite and nourish inspiration.

Jane's egoic needs are:

1. Acceptance
2. Order
3. Independence

When Jane uses her egoic needs to navigate experiences instead of following her standards, she tends to focus on outcomes and organization rather than the quality of the experiences for herself and others. This results in losing the inspiration of human potential and ignoring her possibilities of inspiring others.

She then intellectualizes what she is doing and can get stuck on how it is being accepted and judged. If she becomes consciously aware that she is responding from her needs, she has only to remind herself of her standards and her purpose, especially her passion about potential and inspiration. She can then return to these standards to quiet her ego-mind and choose her purpose and mission in her interactions with other people and in who she is being.

Bob R.

Bob's vision is: Each day is a new opportunity to create loving connections to what is most important in life.

Bob's purpose is: To make it easier for people to have loving connections to what and who are most important to them.

Bob's mission is:

1. To support and participate in groups that easily connect people to what they love.

2. To encourage people to connect to each other with love and kindness.
3. To design and present materials and programs for parents to honor what is most important through their connections.

Bob's gifts are:

1. Creative Connector
2. Safety Provider
3. Process Smoother

Bob's standards include:

1. *Relationships* are grounded in connections. Honoring those connections honors each person and deepens relationships.
2. *Self-knowledge* is the loving gift brought to all relationships. Everything is possible and resolvable through this self-knowledge.
3. *Safe environments* are open, honest, supportive, and caring ones for individuals to take risks and grow personally and collectively.

Bob's egoic needs are:

1. Approval
2. Control

3. Connection

When Bob relies on his needs instead of his standards, he tends to focus on how he plans and organizes activities with an eye to how others will like it. This can lead to feeling pressured to make everything perfect and have every detail covered.

His egoic needs drive his relationships with him focusing on what he needs and wants and how he can get it. This can be in conflict with his purpose and make others feel that he is attempting to control them.

Aware of the responses of other people to his needs-driven behaviors, he is able to choose differently by reminding himself of the importance of relationships and honoring his connections within them. He centers himself by focusing on a safe environment for himself and others to connect and how he can make that easier for everyone.

Kate C.

Kate's vision is: People can be happy and successful only when they pursue and live their dreams.

Kate's purpose is: To bring together people, materials, and support so people can experience and live their dreams.

Kate's mission is:

1. To bring the strengths and wisdom of people together.
2. To provide experiences for instant success, on which confidence can be built.
3. To share knowledge and strategies for people to know their dreams and live them.

Kate's gifts are:

1. Bridge Builder
2. Experience Organizer
3. Dream Explorer

Kate's standards include:

1. *Lifelong learning* increases the possibilities for living dreams and having fulfilling experiences. Every experience can be a learning experience.
2. *Confidence* is the knowledge of what has been achieved and is possible. With confidence, all risks are only expanded opportunities.

3. *Independence* is the freedom to determine success by taking responsibility for choices and behavior.

Kate's egoic needs are:

1. Validation
2. Influence
3. Consistency

When Kate relies on her needs rather than her standards, she looks for ways to expand the reach of her work to receive more validation. This leads to pushing herself to do more in order to have a greater influence. She becomes afraid that her dreams for her work will not translate into how she does her work. She fears that other people will see her and her work as invalid and inconsistent. She may even seek others she can work with to extend her reach and validate her dreams.

When she becomes aware of her needs-driven responses, she takes time to refocus herself and return to the independence of her work, her dream of lifelong learning, and her mission of helping other people live their dreams, too.

After reviewing these examples, take another look at your life plan, make any changes necessary, and rewrite it below:

My life vision is . . .

My life purpose is . . .

My life mission is . . .

My gifts are . . .

My standards are . . .

My needs are . . .

You have a plan and you are ready to let it guide you as your compass for daily living. Hopefully by now, discovering and exploring this plan has already resulted in changes in your life, work, and relationships. You probably recognize when you have been on the path following the plan and when you have wandered away from it. Congratulations, this is not an easy process and at times it can be mystifying, but you have made it through and have discovered a powerful purpose and meaning for your life.

Now get a new 3x5" index card and write your vision, purpose, mission, and gifts on one side. On the reverse side, write your standards and needs. Take the card with you wherever you go and read it often. Especially refer to your card and review your plan whenever you are aware that you are having or have had a negative emotional response in a situation.

You will get better at recognizing how the situation occurred and what you could have said, done, thought, felt, chosen, or decided that would have resulted in a more favorable result. You will also have positive experiences where you can see how you followed your plan—especially your standards—in your choices and responses.

Your emotions will be a great barometer for the pressure inside of you. The more you trust them to warn you when you are wandering from the plan or to affirm when you are following the plan, the easier it will be to lovingly continue on the path to your joy. Best of all, the ego-mind, discussed previously with some trepidation, will over time become a willing partner in reminding you to get back on the path and remember your plan.

The more aware you become of the dance between who you are and the identity the ego-mind provides, the easier it will be to discern which is guiding you. You will know that you have the power to choose to continue to follow your compass, or to return to it when you have wandered away and the ego-mind has taken the lead.

This will be done gently and even with humor as you find yourself talking to your ego-mind and reminding it of your intentions and the guidance you need. Of course, the ego-mind will also be ready with your egoic needs just in case, but more and more it will become a powerful partner in helping you live your best life.

Take a few weeks to expand your awareness, make choices, and explore how you can follow your plan as a compass for daily living. Then come back to *The Guide* and continue through the last section. There, tips and explanations will help you use your plan to live a life of joy with loving relationships you cherish, passionate work that inspires you, and days rich with meaning.

Stop here and live your plan for a few weeks to see where it guides you. Notice when you wander away from it. You will then be open to the tips and suggestions in the last section of the book.

Life on the Path

Your life plan is the great secret of the intended purpose and meaning of your life. Knowing this secret increases your freedom to choose from unlimited possibilities. This concluding section of *The Guide* provides tips and principles to make living on the path of your plan easier and more fulfilling.

There is also a special section addressing the biggest reason most people want to know their life plan—to discover the passionate work or career that will make them happy. Please don't skip to the section on work until you have completed the material before it.

Using your plan as a compass to guide your life, you were promised that you would attract the experiences, relationships, and resources needed to surround yourself with joy and love. This is your intended life, living the new reality distinguished by powerful experiences. Each day on the path will affirm who you truly are and the purpose and meaning of being who you are.

Living on the Path is an Act of Courage

This is not the traditional type of courage defined as bravely confronting difficulty or danger and making sacrifices in the face of opposition. Rather, this is the "courage of your convictions," where your convictions are grounded in love and joy. This is the courage to be the real you, not the egoic you.

The real you knows the meaning of living your purpose in the service of the world. You have the courage of knowing your gifts and how to use them to share your vision in your work and interactions. The courage to be you is all you can be, no matter how many people question, doubt, or dismiss the real you.

Whether alone or in a group, your choices and behavior are congruent with who you are, even when it may seem to disadvantage you. In the long run you know that the best and right choices are the only ones you can make, and the results of those choices confirm your courage.

Living on the Path is the Power of Your Intentions

This is not the traditional concept of goal setting, project planning, and action taking. Intentions are the energy vibrations created by your thoughts and feelings. Every repeated thought and feeling is a magnet for the people, situations, and even objects that match those thoughts and feelings; this is how the *Promise* works.

Whether you knew your life plan or not, your intentions were creating your life and experiences because you attracted those experiences. Knowing and living your plan, your thoughts and feelings will be focused on and directed to what is joyful and loving. That focus attracts the people, situations, and objects that match your intentions, meaning even more joy and love for you, your work, and other people.

Your life plan is the intention for your life and it is through your intentions that the world will experience who you are as you serve others. This is your power to create through your plan and your intentions, with the *Promise* drawing to you what powerfully matches your intentions.

Living on the Path is Choosing Alignment

This is not the traditional balance of time or resources that results in some mathematical equivalence. This is the alignment of who you are, who you are being, and what you are doing with the intended purpose for your life. Choosing relationships, experiences, and work that will support your alignment comprises the most powerful choices you make each day.

Anything or anyone not supporting this alignment will divert you from the power of the *Promise* inherent in your life plan. You won't want to be around people and in situations that divert you from your path because doing so will cause stress, struggle, and unhappiness as your ego-mind conforms to the false identity and egoic reality that matches such negativity.

Alignment with your plan brings peace, calmness, and confident knowing. As you follow your plan, the difference between alignment and ego-identification will become clearer and more obvious through how you feel and what happens around and to you.

Living on the Path is Embracing Change

This is not embracing change as a sacrifice or loss of something you care about or enjoy. With every choice, something is changed. When you embrace any change—even if it was not what you intended or desired—you will experience the power to choose as the power to change anything and everything.

Through the repetition of choices, patterns are created. Patterns repeated become habits, which are automatic choices. The choices from your purpose, standards, mission, and gifts create new patterns, new habits, and automatic choices.

You know who you are going to be and what you are going to do every day, without fear or hesitation. You know nothing can happen that you cannot respond to and get positive results. You will express yourself by aligning with your plan, and that will consistently transform or permanently change your life, relationships, and work through the power of your best and right choices.

Living on the Path is Fueled by Appreciation and Gratitude

This is not the traditional thank-you and acknowledgement of a gift or blessing. This appreciation and gratitude means honoring what connects you to the world by sharing your vision, being your purpose, and doing your mission.

You express your appreciation to people who support and honor your purpose with their efforts and energy. You are grateful for all the opportunities and experiences that enter your life each day without exception. You recognize that knowing your plan reveals every experience as either a part of your plan or a warning that you have wandered away from your plan. You are grateful for the affirmations and the messages.

You appreciate the direction, tools, and guidance of your life plan to address anything that happens while empowering you to create what will happen next. You are grateful for the sacred gift of your unique plan and the endless opportunities to live it in the service of others.

Living on the Path is Living in Flow

This is not sitting back, hoping, and wishing for what you want, while at the same time fearing you won't get it. Struggling, working at it, or making things happen is not required. In fact, these traditional approaches to life will prevent you from trusting, aligning, and flowing through your plan.

Knowing your plan and the *Promise* is to know that everything has a flow that aligns with what is intended. All you have to do is join that flow by trusting where the plan guides and the path leads. The rhythm and timing is built into your plan so you can't rush or hurry it. Choose from your standards, use your gifts, and do your mission; what is necessary for success will be on the way. It will all arrive at the precise moment and in the precise way for you to share your vision and express your purpose through love and with joy.

Living on the Path is Living with Reverent Confidence

This is not the traditional confidence of superiority by comparison to someone or something, or the mastery of skills or knowledge. Confidence is always what is known, not what is wished or hoped for. This is the confidence that comes from knowing that there is a plan for you and your life, work, and relationships with a *Promise* of full support.

This confidence means following your life plan in ways that respect and honor it. The result is a serene and peaceful confidence that requires no explanation, approval, or permission. It is a deep and complete knowing of what is best and right, with you choosing it and living it. From this quiet confidence springs self-trust. Fear no longer drives behavior because reverent confidence guides the next action and behavior without hesitation. You just know.

Living on the Path is the Joy of Living Rather than the Fear of Dying

There is little living when you are waiting to die. Fearing death is a powerful limiting belief that leads to seeking to get as much as possible into the time before that inevitable physical death. Your life plan has no ending or death.

Your legacy of how you lived on the path will continue even after you physically die. Your daily choices, relationships, and work were always intended to share joy and love, and that will continue without you. Those with whom you have shared your vision will continue sharing it on your behalf through their lives and possibly their personal life plans.

Once your piece of the life puzzle is locked in, it can't be removed. It melds into the life puzzle forever. It was never dependent on your physical presence. Your joy of living was communicated by who you were being, and that is permanent.

Living on the Path is Living in the Present

It is an illusion that you have a past that matters and a future with more meaning. All that matters and has meaning is in the present moment. Your point of power is where all choices are made, and the only time they can be made is now.

Your ego-mind may tell you to avoid repeating the past or to worry about the future, but the compass guiding your life path has no past or future; it points in the best and right direction now. The past is filled with regret and attachment to what was or what could have been. The future is filled with the fear of possibilities unknown. Learn from the past, choose in the present, and know the field of possibilities will always be available.

Your plan and the *Promise* make that clear. The beauty of your plan is its enduring presence: whether you knew it or not, it was there to be followed. When you know and follow the plan, the *Promise* is fulfilled now.

Even when the ego-mind is leading, the plan is there, calling you to return to it. Look only to your compass and you will know what to choose now and always. As Oprah Winfrey—who knows the plan for her life—has said, "Doing the best at this moment puts you in the best place for the next moment."

Living on the Path is Living in Integrity

Your life and your legacy will be defined and remembered by your integrity. In *The Guide*, the concept of best and right choices was prominent as the result of following your life plan or compass. Follow the path your compass directs, and you will live a life in integrity defined by making best and right choices or decisions in all situations. Being in integrity is:

- Keeping your word. Doing what you say you will do without exception.
- Being honest at all times by speaking your truths. Your life plan and the choices you make using your standards are your truths.
- Taking absolute responsibility for your choices, actions, and behaviors. No blaming, no rationalizing, and no excuses are used to explain or justify what you have chosen. Responsibility leads to accountability for all responses—*all* responses.
- Being your life purpose and standing where your standards direct you without apologies or guilt. It is the only place you can stand.

The integrity of any structure lies in its strength to withstand pressure and adversity. Your life plan is the structure for your life. Your integrity will be the strength to withstand the inevitable and sometimes daunting challenges in your work, relationships, and daily living.

Without integrity, your life plan is just another plan. Integrity makes your plan a powerful force that can change the world through your courage, intentions, alignment, changes, gratitude, flow, confidence, living, and presence.

Living on the Path is Co-Creating

Co-creating is not the traditional way of creating something new. Co-creating is collaborating with something or someone to bring possibilities into the current reality.

At the beginning of *The Guide*, your life plan was defined as your potential, not your destiny. Knowing and following your life plan will open up all that is possible for you and through you. By following the guidance of your plan, you become a co-creator with the source of your plan.

The purpose of your life is to live in love with joy and to share your love and joy with the world. Love and joy have already been created by your source. All you have to do is align your life, work, and relationships with your plan and you will receive that love and joy. That is The Promise and you become a co-creator through it.

Co-creating your life is co-creating love and joy in every moment and through every choice. Nothing is more powerful or so sacred. Living on your path is *being* love and joy.

Ten Tips for Living Your Life on the Path

 Knowing your life plan and following its guidance should provide a smooth path to love and joy, but sometimes it doesn't. Whatever resistance you encounter inside or outside yourself, and whatever frustration you experience won't be because the plan is flawed or you are not following it effectively. These hindrances will be the direct result of aligning your daily living with a false reality parallel to your new reality of love and joy.

Reality is defined as what is real or true; but a false reality is something which only *appears* to be real or true. Perceived realities limit what most people call "living," and control how they live and work with others and with society.

Knowing these parallel realities will help you recognize when you are aligning with one of them versus aligning with the reality of joy and love intended for you. The only true reality is living your life plan. Mark Twain, the plain-talking American author, could have been describing how easily we align with these other realities when he said, "The trouble with most of us is that we know too much that ain't so."

The World Reality

The majority of the world (especially the people closest to you) probably won't know of life plans, including yours or theirs. Many of them will not understand your commitment to, and focus on, your plan. This means that once you know the plan for your life and consciously begin following it, you will hear a lot of skeptical comments and questions about your "reality."

This can be frustrating and intimidating, especially if you begin to question whether you even have or deserve to have a life plan, let alone whether you should follow it. Sometimes you will feel temporarily confused and pressured to conform.

The world reality or external guidance for life is composed of strong belief systems (mostly limiting ones) and stories that are ingrained in cultural traditions and mores. These beliefs and stories have been very productive and useful for the development and continuation of societies. But they have also kept people from the very personal plans for their own lives and from living as they truly were intended to live. The cost has been the loss of their confidence, their happiness, and especially the love and joy of living their plans.

Social institutions (schools, families, religions, communities, political establishments, and media and entertainment industries) perpetuate this false reality using powerful rewards and punishments. When that doesn't work, the influential people within these social institutions encourage alignment with another parallel reality, the egoic reality (see below). This leads to the same result: people living according to external guidance rather than the internal guidance of who they are.

The result for the rest of us has been the loss of the creations, interactions, and relationships of people who would have been living the plan for their lives. We have missed the joy and the love they could experience and give to us. Instead, we experienced the fear, disappointment, and longing that the world and egoic realities created and are still creating today.

Are you living the world reality, or are you living the egoic reality? It is important to know, especially if you want to live your new reality of love and joy that your life plan is directing you to live.

The Egoic Reality

As the sixth component in your life plan, the ego-mind was your default plan. Ready to lead when you didn't know your plan or wandered from it, your ego-mind kicked in rapidly to accommodate the egoic society surrounding you. This society hooked your attention from the day you were born and was effective because you knew nothing else, least of all the plan for your life.

The egoic reality views life as a process of doing, having, and getting. This includes everything from money to possessions, relationships to marriage, and labels to legacies. You were consistently reminded that life was about challenges, problems, and difficulties, all to be conquered and controlled. Failure was to be avoided by successfully managing, conforming, and achieving in society.

The egoic view said life is a test; pass the test and you will be rewarded. Fail the test and you will be punished. In the egoic reality, life could be summed up as pain versus pleasure.

These two parallel realities, world and egoic, are not a test or a curse. Actually, they serve to remind you of who you are and are not; your potential or diminished potential in living; and that you could or could not have a vital piece of the life puzzle to share with the world. They provide the perfect place for the ego-mind to function as well.

All of it is necessary and helpful. You will navigate these two realities with your compass while using your new reality of love and joy as your home. In the new reality, you will love life and experiences, freely choose powerful experiences, and compassionately interact with other people. Each day will be a gift, an adventure rich with possibilities and surprises.

When you are aware that you have wandered into the world or egoic realities, you will remember your home: the new reality of love and joy, the reality of your life plan, and your purpose in the world.

Here are ten tips that can help you align with, and live your new reality of love and joy—especially when the world and egoic realities seem easier and more comfortable. You will want to refer to these tips often, whether you have wandered off your path or are perfectly aligned with it. They will affirm your life plan and remind you to remember who you really are.

Life Plan Tip #1— Follow the Circle

Throughout *The Guide*, you were asked to repeat and rewrite the components of your life plan. This was done to keep the components flowing through each other because following your life plan is a circular path.

While the components are best discovered in the order they are presented in this book, once your life plan is complete there is no longer a beginning or an end to the components. They are dynamic, interdependent, and constantly expanding. There has never been a square compass, and the compass for your life is like every other: 360° of direction with an unlimited horizon.

However, even as the arrow pivots to point in any direction, the center of your compass remains. This center is you. No matter what choices you make, directions you choose, or path you follow, the center will remain. Trust your compass, whatever direction you are facing. It will always point in the best and right direction for you to go next.

Life Plan Tip #2— Drop the Illusions

Your ego-mind's default plan operates by relying on egoic needs framed by limiting beliefs. These needs and limiting beliefs are strengthened and reinforced by cultural illusions, which are tools of the egoic and world realities.

An illusion is an untruth (lie) appearing to be a truth. Anything that doesn't apply to everyone, all the time, without changing, is an illusion. A truth is always true.

Most of the illusions of a culture change often. They apply to some people and not others; to certain situations and not others. Conditioned by the culture, such illusions are extremely convincing. They are repeated and rewarded by social institutions such as school, families, religion, government, and groups. But they are not truths. These illusions only seem true because everyone believes them without question. Anyone who does question them is labeled or ostracized.

Even when illusions create so much misery and unhappiness in people's lives, they don't question the illusions; they question themselves. They feel guilty and often angry with themselves for not adequately living the illusions they have been told they should be living. They conclude that they cannot trust themselves, their choices, or the calling of their hearts.

Truths are usually the opposite of the illusions. But illusions are so powerful that the truth itself may seem to be the illusion. This often makes discernment of truth and choices from truth difficult. It will be easier when you can identify illusions and recognize the truths they are hiding. The truths will fit your plan, especially your vision and standards. The illusions will fit your egoic needs.

The biggest illusion the ego-mind relies on is that of finding happiness. This powerful and easily believed illusion blocks your path to joy and love because it is grounded in obtaining and owning things and garnering achievements. When this happens, the illusion says you will be happy. Yet, when the symbolic focus of this happiness is achieved or obtained, the ego-mind only sees more to obtain, own, and achieve.

The truth is that happiness is a current and temporary state of satisfaction and contentment, not something you move towards or reach. Follow your life plan, and happiness will be a common experience resulting from who you are being, not what you are doing and getting. It will be repeated over and over again, as part of your joy and love.

What other illusions are serving as your truths? Common ones include getting and using money as the ultimate success; the appearance and care of the body as personal value; security and romance in relationships as the purpose of intimacy; and prosperity and winning at the expense of other people as the value of competition.

When you feel stuck, discouraged, or stressed, look for the illusion your ego-mind is relying on to support your limiting beliefs and fears in response to current situations. What do you believe that isn't true? What do you know to be true? The focus on what is true is the great question that will change your thinking by leading toward truths and away from illusions.

When you recognize an illusion, look for its opposite and you will find the truth. The truths—your truths—are a critical aspect on the path of your life plan. You will come to treasure truth, especially when you recognize when illusions are blocking your path and truths can spotlight your path.

Life Plan Tip #3—
Get Off the Timeline

If the path for following your life plan is a circle, then there can't be a timeline. Often people begin looking for their personal plan because they are unhappy, unsettled, and discouraged. They want to know what they should be doing, and they want to know *now* so they can end the pain and frustration they feel and get moving forward again.

This is based on the illusion that life is progressive (egoic reality). Wherever we are in our lives, we should be learning, doing, and having what will move us further along an imaginary timeline between birth and death. The truth is that our lives continue each day and each moment with new opportunities to choose what our lives will be now. We are not confined by the past or restrained by the future.

While the illusion focuses on progression, the truths in your life plan have no progression and do not follow any line. Your life plan is a circle, as is your intended life. Knowing your life plan and using it as a compass will move you to points along the circle. At these points you'll be expressing your purpose, only to return again later for greater expansion.

While life experiences provide inklings and clues to your life plan, there is no set timeline for knowing it or living it. It is true that the sooner you know your plan, the sooner you can live it—but that depends on you, not the calendar or the clock. The full scope of the plan is revealed as you discover it and it guides your choices and days. Opportunities to share your vision, express your purpose, and do your mission will present themselves when you are ready to greet and choose them.

Additionally, the truth about time is that there is no time except now. You will experience this powerful presence when you are expressing your purpose and using your gifts. These experiences, tasks, and moments will feel timeless, marked by the joy of being in them. Each moment is an invitation to express and experience your plan at a deeper and wider level, which means more and more love as you go around and around the circle.

Life Plan Tip #4— Look Under the Flags

Negative emotions are the physical manifestations of thoughts. Your heart rate and breathing increase, you feel a pit in your stomach, or your hands perspire.

Your mind seems to be racing, and your attention is distracted. It is all a manifestation of the thoughts, interpretations, and beliefs within your ego-mind. A negative emotional response is particularly likely to be an ego-mind experience.

Your emotions are only flags signifying that thought has occurred. The flags immediately go up when the mind engages the experience and sees that responses are needed to protect and defend your identity. You are not usually aware of this mind-body connection until the emotions are strongest or after the experience ends.

Yet, these emotional responses are constant and even chronic. They are important here because your negative emotions and the responses to them block the responses and choices for following your life plan. Negative emotions are always a clear indicator that the ego-mind is in control and its tools, the egoic needs, are driving your responses.

The ego-mind stores memories—especially negative ones—with an emotional charge. The mind uses this to instantly recall memories, interpret new experiences, and identify possible responses for current situations. The emotional charges of thoughts or experiences that were unpleasant or threatened your personal identity and sense of reality now activate negative emotions such as anger, fear, sadness, and guilt.

There are emotional charges for positive memories, too. The most prominent of those positive emotions is the purpose of your life: to live in love and joy. These flags or positive emotional responses are signals of alignment between your ego-mind and your life plan.

Looking under the flags tells you that you are either following your life plan (positive emotions) or following your ego-mind's plan (negative emotions). We are going to focus here on the negative emotions because they confirm a shift from your life plan or new reality to the egoic reality. They may even block a return to your personal life plan.

The problem with negative emotions is that it's so easy to identify with them and conclude that they are the experience we are having. Remember, emotions are only flags waving with the intensity of the charge they represent. They signal the thoughts or interpretations that are their sources. Negative emotions are not the experience, but merely an indication that the experience is being processed by the ego-mind.

When you are feeling negative emotions, look behind them for the thoughts, beliefs, needs, or illusions that sent the emotional flag flying. If you know the source of your negative emotions, they lose their charge and their power to influence or dictate your responses. When you know your interpretations and identify the needs, beliefs, or illusions they represent, you also have the power to choose a different response. You then control the flags and the source of the flags—your thoughts.

In order to follow your life plan, you have to recognize emotional flags, look behind them, and choose to use your standards, gifts, and purpose to respond to your experiences differently. When you are on the path of your plan, your emotions will be more neutral and positive. You will feel the positive emotions of love, joy, and compassion for yourself and others, even in the most challenging circumstances.

Like the flags of negative emotions, you will see these positive flags and know that you are living your plan and your ego-mind has joined you there. This is the ultimate wholeness of who you are and who you are being. You are experiencing life as you were intended to experience it. You are following your plan using all of your resources, including your ego-mind and the flags that are flying high.

Life Plan Tip #5— Ignore the Detours

Expectations and assumptions are another part of the ego-mind's plan for organizing experiences. They can be strong detours from living on the path of your life plan. Together, the past (assumptions) and the future (expectations) become useful tools that the ego-mind relies on when interpreting a current experience. This gives you a false sense of controlling the experience and its outcomes.

The ego-mind aligns with an egoic or world reality using expectations to preserve your identity. Expectations support limiting beliefs by predetermining what will happen and what it will mean. This is an effective detour that can seem like a reasonable approach to the anticipation of situations and interactions.

Expectations are the ultimate setup for the ego mind. They feel safe and logical, but they always lead to either disappointment or relief: disappointment that expectations were not met, or relief that they were. This setup for experiences is used over and over again, holding self-esteem, relationships, and careers hostage. All of it is characterized by changing dynamics and even dramatic encounters described as "living life."

Assumptions are also detours from your life plan. Assumptions are ingrained beliefs and combinations of beliefs that are used to give meaning to experiences. They are based on previous experiences and educated guesses about what could happen, is happening, or may have happened before. The ego-mind uses them as shortcuts for choosing responses (thoughts, feelings, words, actions, and behaviors).

Assumptions provide a false but convincing interpretation of the present. When combined with expectations, an amazingly powerful reality is created that can easily ignore facts. It is all about what you expected or assumed would or did happen, rather than what really did or didn't happen. The mind then chooses responses and choices that match the assumptions and expectations. These detours and the world or egoic realities they align with are then repeated and life happens.

Always question your expectations and assumptions because neither supports living your life plan. By directing your experiences, expectations, and assumptions, the ego-mind maintains that "real world" feel and keeps the world and egoic realities in control. To remove them, you must be open and fully present in situations and interactions. Allow and accept what is happening. Focus on productive and effective responses arising from your life purpose.

Questioning the validity of your expectations and assumptions is an awakening. Free from the attachment to what you or others expect or assume, you gain more power to make conscious choices that are consistent with your life purpose and standards. This is real freedom—the freedom to be who you are and to allow what passionately unfolds. Best of all, delightful surprises become regular experiences without the interference of expectations and assumptions.

Life Plan Tip #6— Fulfill Your Egoic Needs

In the previous ego-mind component of your life plan, it was stated that egoic needs supplant standards when you follow your ego's plan rather than your life plan. Egoic needs come forward quickly and unconsciously to drive your responses before you can consider those that would best fit your purpose and intentions.

By now, you may have accepted the existence and power of your egoic needs as part of your life plan. You may also have hoped to keep them at bay, and even to keep them quiet. Egoic needs are like obstinate little children, always ready to demand that your experiences be about them. They seem to scream, "me, me, me."

Egoic needs can be quieted and modified to become less like children and more like helpful companions. The key is to greatly reduce their fears and thus, their power. This is called getting them fulfilled. It is the most effective way of reducing the impact of your egoic needs on your responses.

Your needs will never go away (they are necessary for the ego plan). But the more the ego-mind is supporting your life plan, the less it will depend on needs to drive your responses. So the combination of knowing and following your plan and reducing the fears driving your egoic needs invites the ego-mind to willingly and even lovingly support the path of your life plan.

Fulfilling your egoic needs is an ongoing process involving three steps that can be repeated. With each step, the fear driving a need is reduced as the longing of the ego-mind for what is missing decreases. Use of your egoic needs to protect your identity and reality is also reduced, allowing you to rely on your standards to guide what is best and right for you in any situation.

Step One—Consciously recognize and reflect on the way your egoic needs are being fulfilled now.

This conscious recognition reduces the perception of the ego that something is missing or lacking. All three of your core egoic needs were already being fulfilled, yet the ego-mind continued to see what was missing; what was separate from you; and what was threatening to your identity. These three views of self and experiences kept the ego-mind active and illusional. A conscious recognition of fulfillment can change these views.

For example, consider your egoic need for approval (the one you have in common with everyone else). Think about the people who currently provide you with approval. Contemplate the many ways they show it in what they say and do.

The most obvious relationship is your most intimate one, such as a spouse, partner, best friend, parent, or sibling. This person listens to you and confides in you; gives you gifts; invites you to share experiences together; and encourages and supports you. He or she provides you with constant, loving approval.

If the people in your life didn't approve of you, they would have left, taken another direction, or found someone or something they approve of more. They are still in your life, so obviously they approve of you. That means you are not being rejected, which is the fear driving the need for approval.

Even when you thought they were rejecting you, they weren't, or else they wouldn't still be around. If you expect or expected them to show their approval in other ways than they do or did, you have taken a detour (see Tip #5). Your fear has been caught up in expectations and assumptions. You have aligned with the egoic or world realities.

Your need for approval is also being fulfilled by what you create, how you interact with other people, the work you do, and your compassion and kindness toward others. As can be seen with the example of the need for approval, you wouldn't be doing and enjoying any of this without the approval of others.

This first step of conscious recognition often proves that any need-driving behavior is pretty much already being fulfilled. Now look at your other two egoic needs and consider how they are already being fulfilled.

Much of what you thought was missing wasn't really missing at all. When you see that current level of fulfillment, you will feel a sense of relief. You will also feel somewhat free from the fears that have been driving those needs and making you unhappy. That is a solid start to having your egoic needs fulfilled.

Now move on to Step Two, where you can further your needs fulfillment.

Step Two—Recognize your responsibility in fulfilling your own needs.

In our society, we have been taught that our needs can only be fulfilled from the outside, usually through other people. So we use our time, make decisions, and limit our possibilities in continual pursuit of fulfillment from people, experiences, and things. There aren't enough people, experiences, or things to fulfill our egoic needs. Even if there were enough, our ego-minds would keep us seeking more.

This is because egoic needs are driven by powerful fears and limiting beliefs. Consider your need for approval again. If you don't approve of yourself, how will you get enough approval from other people, situations, or experiences to counterbalance your own lack of approval? If you don't enjoy who you are, what you can do, and how you do it, you cannot approve of yourself. The more you approve of yourself, the less you will seek the approval of others.

This responsibility to fulfill your own egoic needs from within—especially the need for approval—

depends on how much you focus on what you can do and have done, and not on what you can't do or haven't done. It is vital that you focus on the qualities and characteristics of who you really are and have been (life purpose). This is what brought you love and joy and allowed you to share it with others.

We have been conditioned to feel that we are being selfish when maintaining our self-approval through self-care, personal experiences, and thoughts. We easily set aside our own needs in order to make other people happy. We show our approval of them and then feel guilty for not approving of ourselves enough to say no to them.

Let go of the limiting belief perpetuated by society that to focus on who you are, have been, can do, and have done is being cocky or even selfish. It is a myth that confidence grows from overcoming weaknesses and perceived defects. The origin of confidence is always what you know about your capacity and capabilities—not what you fear or the capacity you hope to have.

Honor, respect, and acknowledge what you know is true about yourself and you will have your personal approval. This self-approval will raise your confidence and further diminish your need to have external validation through the approval of others. This look inward and acknowledgement of what you have done and are doing applies to all your egoic needs, not just approval.

Look at your other two egoic needs. Can you enhance their fulfillment through your self-care, affirmations, experiences, and thoughts? If you can't answer this question for each of your egoic needs, they will be your nemesis. Those needs will always drive your behavior and have you seeking outside for what is necessary and already known inside of you.

Before going on to Step Three, spend a few days with Step Two. Without the critical fulfillment of your needs by yourself, the other steps can't get them fulfilled.

Step Three—Look outside for experiences to top off fulfillment of a need.

This step may seem contradictory to the last two steps, but it has an important place in the process of fulfilling your needs. After you have recognized the current level of fulfillment and looked inside to fulfill an egoic need, you may still need to top it off with a little outside help.

Let's continue with the example of the need for approval. The commonality of this need makes it tough to keep fulfilled when the people surrounding us constantly need our approval and vice versa. We pull on each other in a frenzy of "me, me, me," draining one another of time, energy, and space.

Fulfilling our need for approval is going to require vigilance, especially with regard to the choices we make to love ourselves. And yes, we will even have to look for a little outside approval to supplement our higher levels of personal approval.

There are ways to top off the need for approval without getting pulled back into fear-driven behaviors. Is there a situation or activity where people would appreciate your contributions, creativity, or interactions? If so, go for it. You will get some outside approval that will support your inner self-approval.

But be careful with this third step. Keep in mind that it is most effective only when the first two steps have fulfilled the need almost completely. This means that ideally it will be minimally necessary or not necessary at all.

If you rely on this step too much, you will exhaust your relationships and experiences in seeking for others to meet your needs. Many relationships actually begin as mutual neediness, as do many work situations. It feels desperate and draining to everyone involved. So seeking outside fulfillment of needs just won't get and keep them fulfilled.

Take some time to use the above three steps to fulfill all three of your egoic needs. By doing so, you can greatly reduce the power of those needs to push aside your standards on your life path. This also decreases the urgency of the ego-mind to push into your experiences and use the underlying fear of your needs to direct choices.

With the ego-mind's sense of urgency reduced, you can easily focus on your life plan. You can effectively choose your daily path with love and joy, without feeling driven to do or have something. You can just be you.

Life Plan Tip #7—
Listen to Your Drummer and Your Drum

We have heard that we should follow the beat of our own drummer; but who is the drummer? When you know your life plan, *you* are the drummer. Your life plan is the drum. It is the only drum you need to make music with your life, and you are the only drummer who can play it.

This is important. It means that as well-intentioned as others are with their advice about how to live your life, you are in control. They don't have your drum and they can't be your drummer. No one knows your life plan but you. And only you can walk the path to which it leads.

This doesn't mean that you should ignore or discount the wisdom and knowledge of others. Accept and appreciate it for what it is: a different opinion or perspective. Then determine how you can or can't use it to support your life plan. Only you can know how to best use the resources available to you.

Be grateful, kind, and loving to others for their intended help . . . and go on beating your drum!

Life Plan Tip #8— Look for the "Wow Factor"

Throughout *The Guide* you were asked to look for resonance as a confirmation, affirmation, and deep emotional connection to a word, choice, or experience. There is an even deeper level of resonance called the "Wow Factor." This occurs when a word, phrase, choice, or action resonates deep within your heart or soul.

It is so powerful that you are amazed and stunned by its intensity. It has a depth of knowing that is so absolute that you immediately know the power of its connection to who you are and what you are doing. It is the perfect resonance between you and the source or creator of your life plan. It prompts in you an immediate "wow."

When this occurs, act on it, enjoy it, and relish its guidance. A calm and peaceful "knowing" accompanies the Wow Factor and affirms who you are being. The more you follow your life plan, the more "wows" you will experience.

Life Plan Tip #9— Trust What You Know

When you don't know the plan for your life, it is difficult to trust yourself. We often distrust ourselves when trust is based on limiting beliefs and egoic needs. That makes trust conditional on the ego-mind's fear-based version of reality and our identity.

The result is the interpretation of experiences as struggles, either-or choices, and stressful challenges. Such feelings and distrust don't exactly inspire self-confidence.

When you know your life plan, you will confidently know what was intended for your life and what is right and best for you at all times. Remember, the purpose of your life plan is to be your compass and guide you daily on a path of joy through love. This will be the source of your confidence and the foundation of your self-trust—what you know to be true for you.

Whenever you doubt or distrust yourself, you will know instantly that you have wandered from the guidance of your plan. Your ego-mind has come in to fill the vacuum and your belief system is taking the lead.

Gently remind yourself and your ego-mind of your plan and the standards for guiding your choices. This simple, conscious prompt returns you to your path. When you feel unsure, it is very helpful to review your

3x5" card for an energized reminder of the power you have to guide your life.

Life Plan Tip #10—
Put Your Mind to It

Another phrase often heard is "put your mind to it." This admonition usually implies that you are not focused or thinking clearly. That sounds sensible, but it will sound different to you in light of your life plan.

If you put your mind to it as you have in the past, your ego-mind will attempt to process the situation, find the logic, determine the labels, and formulate a plan of action. But you don't want the ego-mind to provide the plan. You want your life plan to guide you, and you want to use your mind to support your plan.

When you choose to focus on the guidance of your life plan, you invite the ego-mind to focus on the plan, too. Since your mind always follows your focus, it then becomes a partner on your path. It will remind you of your life plan, which it also knows now.

The ego-mind can be very useful for living your life plan because it holds the memories, images, and knowledge from your previous life experiences. When you invite it to support your plan, the ego-mind provides the wisdom it has accrued.

Keep reminding your ego-mind of your intention to make right and best choices, and it will help you know and choose them. This doesn't mean it won't have its defensive and protective plan ready to go. It will; it always does. In time, it will put that plan on an imaginary shelf at the back of your imaginary memory storage.

It will be there, but it will be rarely used. And even if the ego's plan is used, you will be fully aware that you have relied upon it. You will look for what has distracted or detoured you from your life plan, and make a course correction to get back to your path. The ego will then return its plan to the shelf.

The ego-mind is an important component of your life plan. It is the default plan within your plan, available to be used when you don't know your plan or wander off your path. It is necessary. Embrace your ego-mind as the gift that it is, with the knowledge that it will always be there to help, support, and sustain you.

The ego-mind then becomes the next best thing to your life plan, a supporter, and even a lifesaver at times.

Working Your Life Plan

Knowing your life plan and aligning your work or career with it doesn't mean throwing your previous knowledge, experiences, and skills out the window; that would be a serious mistake. The work that now makes you miserable probably aligned with your life plan at some level at one time and may still do so with some adjustments.

In most cases, it wasn't necessarily a problem with the work. Rather, you probably became distracted from your alignment without realizing it. This can happen when you get a promotion, expanded responsibilities, or a transfer to a different position.

What seemed logical in the world of work may have been an unintended diversion from your life purpose, mission, and using your personal gifts and standards. Your experience and capabilities increased your potential, but that didn't mean you should have increased your workload or diverted from what you were already doing successfully.

Verification that you have moved away from your life plan in your work or career is often manifested by increased stress responses, feeling drained and overwhelmed, and physical diseases and disorders. These are internal warnings that you are off your path. Flow has stopped, and so has the passion that accompanied it.

You are following the ego-mind's plan rather than your life plan. You are surviving rather than thriving. Possibly, you are also numbed by the assumption that your experience with work happens to everyone.

This isn't intended to happen to you or anyone else. What is intended for you is to express your life purpose, do your mission, and use your gifts with passion, love and joy, in your work and every aspect of your life.

To get back on the path of your life plan does not mean leaving your work, changing careers, or sacrificing income or benefits. Remember that the *Promise* provides all that is necessary for you to have abundance when you follow your life plan. Rely on the plan you have discovered in *The Guide* to decide what is necessary now to realign your work or career with your path.

You may only have to restructure your work and your work environment. Maybe a change in the way you think about your work in terms of your standards and recommitting yourself to your work will realign you. Or, you may have to change careers or work situations.

Whatever is necessary, your life plan will guide you there. Get out your 3x5" card and review your life plan. Update it as needed.

Using your plan as your compass, you can follow the steps below. They will help you determine what could be the best choices for your work situation now, ranging from rethinking to restructuring, or from changing environments to changing careers.

Step One—
Know Your Gifts and Your Skills

Take your gifts (see Personal Gifts component) and write each one at the top of a separate piece of paper. Under each gift, list the skills that depend on that gift to be successful.

Skills are actions, tasks, or behaviors that produce a product, experience, or outcome. Some examples might be teaching, organizing, communicating, or assembling. Skills are usually what most people first think of when they are asked about their gifts. They may do these skills well or be very experienced using them, so they easily assume those are their gifts.

There is a big difference between them, especially when it comes to using gifts and skills in a work environment. Remember, gifts don't require knowledge, experience, or training; they are not learned. Your gifts were born with you and you have used them throughout your life. They have helped you to see the world and your experiences in ways that others did not, but which fit your life plan.

Skills are learned and improve with knowledge and experiences. You have to use them to maintain them. Skills derived from personal gifts are the easiest to learn and master. They easily express the passion of the gifts underneath them. Skills not derived from gifts can be learned and even mastered, but they are draining and can become boring.

Let's see how gifts and skills fit together so that you can construct your list of skills derived from your gifts. For example, if the gift is "bridge builder," here are some possible skills that someone who "bridge builds" could do easily and masterfully:

- Sees connections in complex situations or tasks.
- Mediates resolutions or conflicts.
- Finds information needed by someone to solve a problem.
- Sees how parts make up a whole.
- Brings people together on common ground.
- Builds networks of people or things.

Notice that the skills above involved bridge building between people, situations, and even things. And yes, the person could also build real bridges. The list of skills can be quite extensive, and it can be a lot of fun to identify the skills that come from a particular gift.

You will see with your gifts that you have many skills that have already come out of them. And hopefully you will discover even more. Avoid censoring possible skills, especially by using your experience, training, or résumé to eliminate skills as impractical or unrealistic for you.

List all the skills you can think of. Later in this section you will learn what to do with the ones you are unfamiliar with.

When you have skills lists for each gift, move on to Step Two.

Step Two—
Observe Other People While They Work

Who is currently using the skills you have identified for each of your gifts? Pay special attention to the people who seem to love their work and are getting satisfying results using the same skills you listed above. These people are using their gifts and the skills from them to passionately and lovingly share their life vision, express their purpose, and do their mission. They may have similar life plan components to yours.

Talk to these people if you can. An interview is a fun and informative way to find out how and why they enjoy what they do. Ask them how they feel doing what they do and how they see it impacting other people. You can ask them about their life plans, but they likely won't know their personal life plan. They will have clues about it, just like you did. Take some notes on what you learn from them and what they say that resonates with you, especially if it has the "Wow Factor" around it.

If you can't talk to the people you are observing, make notes on what they are doing when they are most joyful, at ease, and having fun. Note the interactions with other people that bring smiles to them and the people with whom they are interacting. This is the clear connection between a person's purpose and gifts and their service to others.

When you have your notes, move on to Step Three. These notes will be valuable clues to how your gifts and skills can benefit other people and create passion for you, too.

Step Three— Narrow Down the Skills for Your Gifts

Consider your personal gifts, skills lists, and the skills you observed in others. Look for the skills that fully utilize your gifts and are deeply joyful and rewarding when you are doing them. You are going to narrow your possibilities.

Identify the professions, occupations, or environments where people with your skills are thriving. You will be attracted to those where you could flourish doing your mission, expressing your purpose, and sharing your vision. Go there and observe, interview, and take notes again.

You will now have some ideas of what work or career could most benefit from your gifts and skills. Reduce your possibilities down to fewer than five occupations, industries, or task areas. Learn as much as you can about them from the Internet or other resources.

Once you are comfortable with the information you have acquired, set it aside. You will return to it later. Now go on to the second part of this step.

Begin applying the gifts and skills clarification to your current work situation. Remember that the work you do now does have a lot of you and your plan in it, especially if you have been doing it for longer than six months.

Can you modify the current tasks, responsibilities, or situations in ways that would better utilize your gifts and allow you to do your mission? If there are parts of your current work tasks or situations that are not you (they are draining), can you delegate them or hire someone else to do them?

There is always someone who has the gifts and skills you don't. Everybody has a piece in the life puzzle, and those spaces are waiting to be filled. Finding those people and helping them follow their life plan while supporting your own plan is truly "a match made in heaven."

Try this combination of narrowing your work down to that which creates passion and then delegating the rest to others. See if the situation improves for you.

Also look for tasks, skills, or activities that you can just stop doing or discard. Letting go of some aspects of a work situation can increase the time, space, and energy you give to work that is really you. Of course, this can only be done if it does not affect the continuing success of yourself and others.

If your try these approaches but still feel drained and see no way to restructure your current work, then you are probably ready for a change. To successfully and efficiently change careers requires a transition.

While continuing your current work, volunteer to shadow someone who is doing the work you are interested in doing. Also, return to the first part of this step for the information you gathered about other work possibilities and start looking for a different situation.

The key to this step is to look for a match between who you are when you are following your life plan and who you want to be in a work environment. It may help to write a narrative describing the ideal work situation where you would be using your gifts and expressing your purpose. Visualize what a day or week in this environment would be like, and especially how it would feel.

It is important to focus on the positive aspects of what you will experience and how you will feel in this ideal work situation. Avoid writing what you don't want, won't be doing, and wouldn't want to feel. Keep the content specific to the ideal. This narrative can be a very effective and powerful tool for helping you clarify your intended work.

Step Four— Seek More Knowledge or Training

This last step is critical before making any major changes in your work environment or career. In the Gifts component of your life plan, it was pointed out that knowledge expands gifts by expanding possibilities, especially for learning new skills. Is there more education, experience, or skills practice that would enhance the skills your gifts could support? If so, you will want to seriously consider taking action here before you make a major work or career move.

Don't worry about the difficulty of learning something new. If the skills match them, your gifts will make learning and mastery easy. Your progress will be rapid.

If you have the resources to comfortably change careers or work as you acquire more training, then you may be able to move on. But if you need the income and benefits you currently have, then you should stay in that job in the interim.

Take the time you need to expand your skills, locate the situation you desire, and make a smooth transition. Some people even like to begin the new work part-time to further assess it.

Because it takes some shaping and adjusting, it is recommended that you follow this process as carefully and comfortably as necessary for you. Remember, you are looking for the work that allows and fully supports who you are and what you are intended to contribute to the world.

When this happens, the work you do will be passionate. You will look forward to doing it and thrive by doing it. Best of all, the entire world will benefit from you doing that work with joy and love.

Work is a major part of our lives, especially in terms of our joy and love. So the work or career that fully expresses our life plan and shares it with others is of vital importance.

If most people knew their intended work and did it, the world would run smoother; their work experience would be more joyful and loving; and the process of creating and producing would benefit both those doing the work and those experiencing the results. Additionally, people would be healthier, wealthier, and a lot wiser.

In order to use your work or career to express your life path, you have to know your life plan. You then have to prepare for and choose work that fully expresses your vision, purpose, and mission.

That work has to be done with the guidance of your standards while fully utilizing your gifts and the skills they support. This is not only the ideal work environment, but it is also the one intended for each of us.

If you only accept or participate in work that allows you to express who you are and make the world better through your work, you could be the next person who says, "I can't believe I get paid to do this!"

Back to the Beginning

You have arrived at the end of the process for knowing your life plan! You should have a full 3x5" index card that you may even have memorized by now.

Your life plan is the secret to the purpose of your life. It is what will give your life meaning.

Using your plan as a compass, you know where to go, what to do, and with whom to do it. However, arriving at the end is really returning to the beginning. You are beginning your life again, learning from your experiences, and knowing what you want to experience currently and in the future.

Your life was intended to be filled with joy and love. You were also intended to share your love and joy with the world.

You were given a plan to serve as a compass to guide you. You have the tools to fully live on the path your life plan inspires.

Your responsibility as a human being is to live your plan. In doing so, you will slide your unique piece of the life puzzle into place for all of us to enjoy. The world will benefit.

Thank you for choosing to be who you are and share yourself with the world. As you do that, you will discover that there is even more to your plan. It is deeper and richer than anything you can imagine. So is the *Promise* that came with your plan.

Everything you need will be provided so that you can continue to expand your plan and experience more joy and love. You will attract all that is possible and necessary to live the best and right life for you. The abundance you attract will guarantee it now. And through your legacy, it will continue long after you die.

Thank you for using *The Guide* to help you. It is recommended that you return to this very personal and unique book many times as you choose your life path. This is your book, the guide to who you are and were intended to be.

The beginning waits for you to come back and learn even more about the plan for your life. There is more—much more.

As you live on the path of your plan, do the exercises again, answer the questions once more, and update the words and focus of your components. Your life plan will get clearer and you will fine-tune it as you discover more specifics for how and what you can do passionately each day.

Live in joy and love and serve the world, for that is the purpose and the meaning of your life and all our lives!